AMAZING

MAYA

INVENTIONS

◆ YOU CAN BUILD YOURSELF ◆

SHERI BELL-REHWOLDT

nomad press

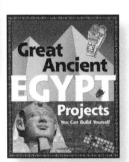

To my twin sister, Jeri,
the "craftiest" person I know.

Nomad Press
A division of Nomad Communications
10 9 8 7 6 5 4 3 2 1
Copyright © 2006 by Nomad Press
All rights reserved.

No part of this book may be reproduced in any form without permission in writing from the publisher, except by a reviewer who may quote brief passages in a review. The trademark "Nomad Press" and the Nomad Press logo are trademarks of Nomad Communications, Inc. Printed in the United States.

ISBN: 0-9771294-6-2

Questions regarding the ordering of this book should be addressed to
Independent Publishers Group
814 N. Franklin St.
Chicago, IL 60610
www.ipgbook.com

Nomad Press
2456 Christian St.
White River Junction, VT 05001
www.nomadpress.net

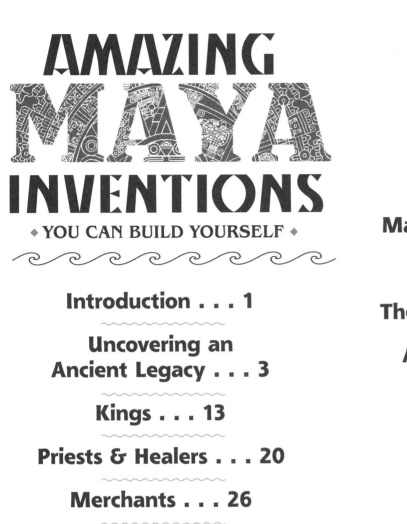

AMAZING MAYA INVENTIONS

♦ YOU CAN BUILD YOURSELF ♦

TABLE OF CONTENTS

The ancient Maya civilization lasted about 3,000 years. Their history is divided into three main time periods: the pre-classic period, the classic period, and the post-classic period. Descendants of the Maya still live in Central America.

3114 BCE: The creation of the world, according to the Maya Long Count calendar.

2600 BCE: The first Maya settlements appear on the Pacific and Caribbean coasts of what is now Mexico, Guatemala, and Belize.

2000 BCE: The rise of the Olmec civilization, which influences the Maya in math, architecture, and astronomy.

2000 BCE–250 CE

PRE-CLASSIC PERIOD

Cities based on farming spread across Mesoamerica, into the lowland rainforests (what is now Mexico, Guatemala, and Belize) and the highland mountains (what is now Guatemala and Honduras).

700 BCE: The Mayan written language is developed.

400 BCE: The earliest known solar calendars are carved in stone.

300 BCE: The Maya adopt the idea of a hierarchical society, which is a society with upper and lower classes ruled by nobles and kings.

100 BCE: The city of Teotihuacán is founded and becomes a religious and cultural trading center.

Teotihuacán

100 CE: For unknown reasons, the Olmec civilization begins to decline.

250 CE–900 CE

CLASSIC PERIOD

Known as the Maya's "golden age." Maya kings rule great cities.

400 CE: Cities in the Maya highlands are taken over by Teotihuacán, which becomes very dominant. Other cities merge together into larger cities called city-states. These city-states fight over land, slaves, and victims for human sacrifices.

500 CE: Teotihuacán is in trouble and many of its citizens flee to Tikal, which becomes the first great Maya city.

600 CE: A mysterious event destroys Teotihuacán. Tikal becomes the largest city in Mesoamerica.

683 CE: At age 80, the greatest Maya king, Pacal dies. He is buried in the Temple of Inscriptions at Palenque.

Temple of Inscriptions

751 CE: Trade between Maya city-states declines and conflict increases.

869 CE: In Tikal, construction stops and the city begins to decline.

899 CE: Tikal is abandoned.

900 CE–1600 CE
POST-CLASSIC PERIOD

The classic period ends as the Maya flee their southern lowland city-states. Possible reasons: drought, too many people, too little food, war, and disease. Maya cities in the northern Yucatán continue to thrive. From as many as 13 million people at its height in 750 CE, by 950 CE more than 90 percent of the Maya population have died.

1200 CE: Northern Maya cities begin to be abandoned.

1224 CE: The city of Chichén Itzá is abandoned, and its people settle outside the city.

Chichén Itzá

1263 CE: The people of Chichén Itzá begin building the city of Mayapán, which becomes the capital of Yucatán.

1441 CE: The people of Mayapán start to leave and it is abandoned by 1461. After this, warring groups compete to rule over the others.

1502 CE: Christopher Columbus learns of the Maya when he captures a Maya trading canoe near the Gulf of Honduras. Word soon spreads across Spain about the riches of Mesoamerica. Conquistadors set out to claim the resources of the land and people, especially their gold, for Spain.

1517 CE: The Spanish arrive on the shores of the Yucatán.

1519 CE: Hernán Cortés

Cortés

begins exploring the Yucatán and the Spanish begin their conquest of Mexico.

1541 CE: The Spanish conquer the Maya and establish a capital city at Mérida in the northern Yucatán.

1562 CE: Diego de Landa, a Spanish bishop, begins to brutally force the Maya to accept Catholicism. He tortures and kills and orders the burning of all Maya books.

1695 CE: The ruins of Tikal are discovered by a Spanish priest, who had become lost in the jungle.

Tikal

1697 CE: The last ancient Maya city, Tayasal, set deep inside the rainforests of what is now Guatemala, falls to conquistador Martin de Ursua.

1843 CE: John Lloyd Stephens and Frederick Catherwood explore Central America looking for Maya ruins. They publish a book of their travels, igniting world interest in the ancient Maya.

1886 CE: Mayan hieroglyphs begin to be catalogued.

1952 CE: Pacal's tomb is discovered at Palenque.

1973 CE: Scholars make breakthroughs in understanding the Mayan written language. Previously only some of the hieroglyphs describing numbers, astronomy, and the Maya calendar were interpreted. Today, 90 percent of the glyph meanings are understood.

1992 CE: A Maya woman wins the Nobel Peace Prize for fighting for human rights for the Maya.

Pacal II, also known as Pacal the Great, or K'inich Janahb' Pakal

Ruler of the great Maya city-state of Palenque for 68 years, from 615 to 683. The name *Pacal* translates to "shield." Pacal II may be the most famous Maya king. He took the throne at age 12 and died at 80. During his reign he built Palenque into an important Maya city. He is buried in a tomb deep within the Temple of Inscriptions, a huge memorial pyramid. After his death he was worshipped as a god.

Kan Bahlam II, Snake Jaguar

The son of Pacal II, he inherited the throne at the age of 48. He continued to add to Palenque's architecture, including three small pyramid temples: the Temple of the Sun, the Temple of the Cross, and the Temple of the Foliated Cross. They were designed to echo the shapes of distant mountains.

Shield Jaguar the Great

King of Yaxchilán, a rival city of Palenque, from 681 to 742 CE. The powerful family of his most important wife, Lady Xok, helped to keep him on the throne for 50 years. A powerful warrior, he brought many other cities under his control. Shield Jaguar died in 742 CE at the age of 92.

Lady Xok of Yaxchilán

The most prominent wife of Shield Jaguar the Great, Lady Xok is shown in many Yaxchilán stone carvings. In one well-known doorway panel, she is shown pulling a thorn-studded rope through her tongue for a blood sacrifice as Shield Jaguar holds a torch over her head. Lady Xoc died in 749 CE.

Waxaklajuun Ub'aah K'awiil, also known as 18 Rabbit

He was the 13th ruler of Copán and one of the city's most famous kings. He ruled from about 695 to 738 CE, when he was captured and sacrificed by a king called Cauac Sky.

Hernán Cortés (1484–1547)

The conquistador who left Spain in 1519 to capture Mesoamerican gold for Spain. Since the Maya had no gold, except for small amounts they had acquired through trade, he and the Spaniards focused more on the Aztec, neighbors of the Maya.

Charles V, King of Spain (1500–1558)

Approved the Spanish conquest of the Americas, after taking the throne in 1516. Charles gave the throne to his son, Philip II, when he decided to enter a monastery. He died 2 years later.

Diego de Landa (1524–1579)

A Spanish priest who tried to convert the Maya to Christianity. He did so in a brutal way. He ordered the burning of the Maya codices, the torture of Maya people, and the demolition of Maya buildings.

John Lloyd Stephens (1805–1852) Frederick Catherwood (1799–1854)

Stevens was an American travel writer and Catherwood was a British artist. They teamed up to locate Maya ruins. During their two expeditions to Mesoamerica, they visited 44 ancient cities before returning home in 1842 to write *Incidents of Travel in Central America*. The book generated much interest among archaeologists, scholars, and the general public.

PLACES TO KNOW

Yucatán Peninsula: The peninsula in Mexico that was once the heart of Maya civilization. There are many Maya archaeological sites throughout the peninsula and many Maya descendents still live there.

Teotihuacán: A city founded in 100 BCE that became a religious and cultural trading center. It was the largest city in the Americas. Around 500 CE, for unknown reasons, many of its citizens began to flee to Tikal. In 600 CE it was destroyed by a mysterious event.

Tikal: The first great city of the Maya civilization. It became important between 500 and 600 CE, as Teotihuacán weakened. Today it is the largest of the ancient ruined cities of the Maya civilization.

Palenque: A great city ruled by Pacal the Great. Palenque contains some of the finest architecture, sculpture, and carvings the Maya ever produced.

Yaxchilán: This was an important city throughout the classic era. Yaxchilán waged war with its rival, Palenque, in 654 CE.

Its greatest power came during the long reign of King Shield Jaguar II, who died in his nineties in 742 CE. Today, Yaxchilán is known for its large quantity of excellent sculptures.

Copán: A strong kingdom established in 159 CE. At its height, it had an unusually wealthy citizenship. As a result, the carvings and sculptured decorations on the buildings of Copán are some of the finest in Mesoamerica.

Uxmal: For generations Uxmal was the most powerful city in western Yucatán, and for a while it was allied with Chichén Itzá and dominated all of the northern Maya area. Not long after 1200 CE, construction at Uxmal stopped, and the city began its decline.

Chichén Itzá: This was a major city during the Maya classic period, around 600 CE. It reached its height after the Maya sites of the central lowlands to the south had already collapsed. Revolt and civil war among the Maya in 1221 CE led to the city's decline and authority over the Yucatán Peninsula shifted to Mayapán.

Mayapán: A pre-Columbian Maya city that was the political capital of the Maya in the Yucatán Peninsula from about the late 1220s to the 1440s. Today the site of Mayapán is not one of the most impressive Maya sites. This is partly because architecture on the scale of Chichén Itzá and other Maya cities was never attempted there.

Tayasal: Located in the southern Maya lowlands, it was the center of the last independent Maya city-state to be subdued by the Spanish, in 1697. Unfortunately, most of the archaeological treasures of this city were lost when it was destroyed and rebuilt by the Spanish after its fall.

Mérida: The modern capital city of the Yucatán state in Mexico. It is located in the northwest part of the peninsula in between the ruins of Chichén Itzá and Uxmal. It was founded in 1542 and was built over the Maya city of T'ho. Some carved Maya stones from ancient T'ho are still visibly reused in Spanish colonial buildings, and some Maya still use the ancient name T'ho when referring to Mérida.

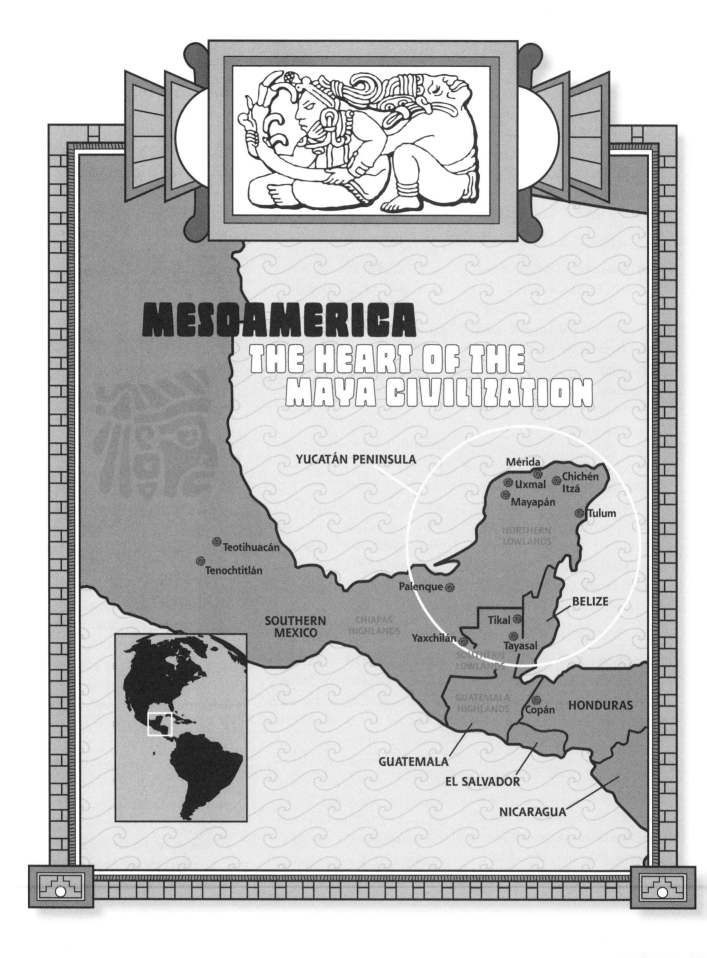

MESOAMERICA
THE HEART OF THE MAYA CIVILIZATION

YUCATÁN PENINSULA

Mérida

Uxmal Chichén Itzá

Mayapán

Tulum

NORTHERN LOWLANDS

Teotihuacán

Tenochtitlán

Palenque

BELIZE

SOUTHERN MEXICO

CHIAPAS HIGHLANDS

Tikal

Yaxchilán

Tayasal

SOUTHERN LOWLANDS

GUATEMALA HIGHLANDS

Copán HONDURAS

GUATEMALA

EL SALVADOR

NICARAGUA

INTRODUCTION

Have you ever thought about what life would be like if you had lived during the time of the ancient Maya, long before the first European explorer set foot in the New World? The ancient Maya people were the most advanced civilization of their time: they were accomplished mathematicians, master builders, and they developed a complex written language. They also created some of the world's most impressive art, in the form of jewelry, carvings, paintings, and ceramics.

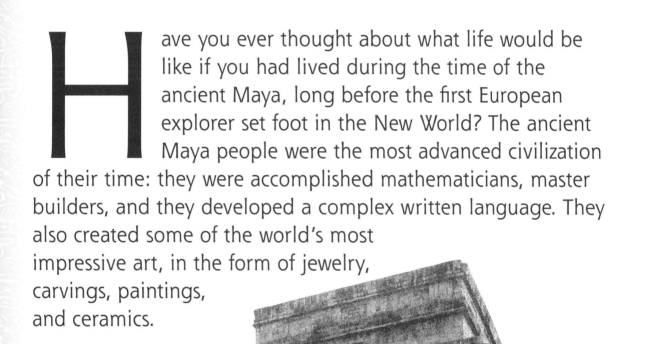

This book will help you learn about the Mayas' complex calendars and a hieroglyph-based writing system, how they raised crops in less-than-perfect soil and created a vast network of huge, complex cities. You'll discover exactly how the Maya people believed their gods created the world's first humans—and how they demanded ceremonial blood sacrifices in exchange for this gift of life! You'll explore how the Maya built towering pyramids from slabs of limestone and carved intricate patterns into hard green jadeite stone without the help of metal tools. And you'll also get an idea of how a normal Maya society worked.

Most of the projects in this book can be made by kids with minimal adult supervision, and the supplies needed for them are either common household items or easily available at craft stores. So, take a step back—way back—into the Maya classic period and get ready to **Build It Yourself**!

CHAPTER 1

UNCOVERING AN ANCIENT LEGACY

D eep in the rainforests of Central America sit the majestic ruins of an Indian people called the Maya (pronounced MYE-uh). They lived in an area of about 125,000 square miles, in what are now the countries of Mexico, Belize, Guatemala, and Honduras. At their peak, as many as 10 million or more Maya lived in this area, which historians call "Mesoamerica."

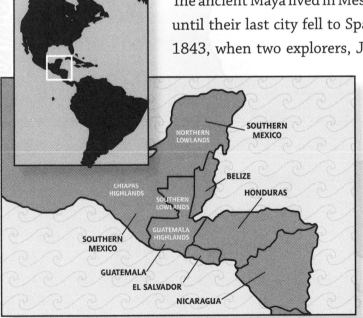

The ancient Maya lived in Mesoamerica for close to 3,000 years, until their last city fell to Spanish invaders in 1697. Yet until 1843, when two explorers, John Lloyd Stephens and Frederick Catherwood, published a book about the Maya ruins, few people were aware that these once-great cities had existed. Since that time, many experts have joined the quest to uncover the history of the ancient Maya. We now know that the Maya were a people of great accomplishment. The

Ruins at Tulum.

ancient Maya were master artists and builders. They were also experts at studying the movements of the planets and stars—and they did so without the telescopes and computers we have today!

In 1839, Stephens, an American travel writer, and Catherwood, a British artist, traveled to Central America after hearing reports of fantastic old ruins. They hired guides with machetes to hack pathways for them through the thick, humid rainforests. Their exploration wasn't easy: it was hot, the mosquitoes were fierce, and curious monkeys howled in the treetops overhead. They also battled malaria, a painful disease caused by mosquito bites.

But Stephens and Catherwood didn't give up, and they knew their persistence had been worth it when they stumbled upon the ruins of the ancient Maya city, Copán. The two men gazed in amazement at Copán's towering stone pyramids and tall, carved stone slabs. These stone slabs are called **stelae**. Maya carvers decorated the stelae with picture symbols called **hieroglyphs**. Scholars now believe that Copán was first settled around 1000 BCE. Amazingly, Stephens was able to buy the ruins for $50 so that he and Catherwood could study them in detail.

DID YOU KNOW?

"Maya" or "Mayan"? The term "Mayan" should be used only when referring to the Mayan language. The term "Maya" should be used when you talk or write about the people and their culture. Maya is both plural and singular.

DID YOU KNOW?

To make his drawings, Catherwood used a drawing device called a camera lucida. This allowed Catherwood to see the object he was drawing and his paper at the same time. He was able to easily trace the outlines of buildings and stelae, ensuring that his drawings were accurate.

A CLOSE CALL FOR CATHERWOOD

It was at the ruins of the Maya city Palenque, in the central lowlands of Mexico, that Catherwood contracted malaria. In humans, the disease attacks red blood cells, causing them to burst. Painful symptoms include fever, shivering, vomiting, and joint pain. People can slip into comas or even die if they don't get medical help. After Catherwood fell ill, he returned to the United States to rest. When he felt better, he went back to Central America with Stephens. On that trip they discovered the Maya ruins of Chichén Itzá and Tulum. When Catherwood got sick again, both men returned to New York and published a book called *Incidents of Travel in the Yucatán*. It described the 44 Maya sites they found during their expeditions.

Catherwood spent many hours sketching copies of the hieroglyphs in his notebooks. He was sure the symbols contained information about Maya life. He was right! When **epigraphers** and **archaeologists** saw Catherwood's drawings, they were amazed. Soon, scholars around the world began to study the ancient Maya. They tried hard to figure out what the symbols meant. They ignited a strong interest in Maya history that continues today.

Catherwood's drawing of a stela at Copán.

WHO WERE THE MAYA?

Though scholars still have much to learn from the glyphs and ruins, they have uncovered enough information for us to answer the question, "Who were the Maya?"

The Maya shared similar religious beliefs, social structures, and building styles to other Mesoamerican cultures like the Olmec and Aztec. But each culture was also unique in just as many ways, which we'll talk about in the following pages.

Experts divide Maya history into three time periods:

- the pre-classic period, about 1500 BCE–250 CE
- the classic period, 250–900 CE
- the post-classic period, about 900–1524 CE.

WORDS TO KNOW

stelae: Vertical slabs of stone that the Maya used to record dates and important information about their rulers. Most are between 3 and 23 feet tall. Maya artists used stone chisels and wooden hammers to carve symbols into the stone.

hieroglyphs: A writing system in which pictures and symbols represent meaning or sounds or a combination of the two. One symbol is called a glyph.

epigraphers: Experts who study ancient writings.

archaeologist: Someone who studies ancient people and their cultures.

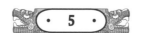

BCE? CE?

What does it mean when dates end with the letters BCE and CE? BCE stands for Before Common Era. The beginning of the Common Era is marked by the birth of Jesus and begins with the year 1 followed by the letters CE. Events that happen before the first year of the Common Era are Before the Common Era. The years BCE may seem backward, because as time passes the years actually become smaller in number. For example, a child born in 300 BCE would celebrate turning 10 in the year 290 BCE. Think of it as a countdown to the Common Era.

Maya society grew from humble beginnings. Long before they lived in great cities, the Maya were simple **nomads**. They roamed the land in small family groups, moving to new areas when they ran out of food. It was only as they learned to harvest **maize** and other crops that they began to settle in the area. They built small villages in the first or second **millennium** BCE (2000–100 BCE). The villages were rough, but they still made for safer and easier living than caves and open camps!

As the farmers spread across Central America, they faced many challenges. In the south, near the highland mountains (now Guatemala and Honduras), they found good volcanic soil in which to grow their crops. But in the northern lowlands of the Yucatán Peninsula, farmers had only two inches of topsoil covering **limestone** bedrock. Yet this scrubby area flowed with many underground streams and wells the Maya called *dz'onot*. The Spanish later called them *cenotes*. The Maya believed these wells led to the **underworld**, the unhappy home of evil gods.

The farmers that settled in the central and southern lowlands were surrounded by thick tropical rainforest. They grew cotton, despite the heavy rains that fell about 7 months out of the year, from May through December. The waters could rise 10 feet or more, swamping the land with mildew. But the animals of the forest, such as monkeys, jaguars, iguanas, deer, turkeys, wild boars, and birds provided the Maya with plenty of food. The Maya who settled along the coast traded salt, turtles, fish, and oysters for crops they did not grow.

Around 500 BCE, the Maya living in the central lowland villages began to rebuild them into great cities. Some of these cities include Palenque, Tikal, and Yaxchilan. Later, the Maya also built cities in the south and east. One of the most impressive is Copán, the first city Stephens and Catherwood found during their exploration. By 50 CE, pyramids, city plazas, and *Pok-A-Tok* ball courts were added to the cities. *Pok-A-Tok* was a ball game in which teams acted out the ongoing battle between good and evil. We'll talk more about *Pok-A-Tok* later on.

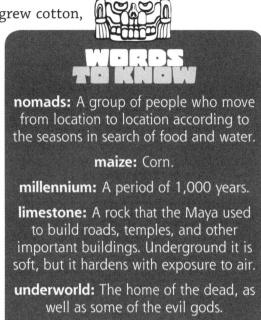

WORDS TO KNOW

nomads: A group of people who move from location to location according to the seasons in search of food and water.

maize: Corn.

millennium: A period of 1,000 years.

limestone: A rock that the Maya used to build roads, temples, and other important buildings. Underground it is soft, but it hardens with exposure to air.

underworld: The home of the dead, as well as some of the evil gods.

Diagram of a *Pok-A-Tok* court.

Ruins at Palenque with the ball court in the foreground.

DID YOU KNOW?

The *memba uinicoob* were the common workers in each city's population, and it was their job to build the city structures and roads. They also built the stone homes of the royals and planted their crops.

Maya glyph for obsidian.

By 300 CE, the cities were occupied by four classes of people. At the top were the kings, priests, and other members of the royal family. In the middle were the merchants and artists. Below them, was the *memba uinicoob*, which means "common worker." The lowest class of people was the slaves, called *pentacoob*. While Maya kings enjoyed unlimited wealth and power, slaves had none.

The ancient Maya were a Stone Age people. This doesn't mean they existed when there were cavemen during the Paleolithic period; it means they did not have metal tools to help them with their daily tasks. Their tools were made of wood, stone, and bone. So, instead of iron-tipped arrows, chisels, knives, axes, and hammers, their wooden tools had blades made from obsidian and flint. Obsidian is a black glass produced by erupting volcanoes, and flint is a very hard grayish black form of quartz. Both could be chipped to make sturdy, razor-sharp blades.

THE MAYA GOLDEN AGE

Even without metal, the ancient Maya were able to accomplish a great deal. We know most about the Maya classic period (250–900 CE),

MAYAN WORDS FOR DIFFERENT GROUPS OF PEOPLE

ajaw: lord.

halch uinic: the leader or king of each Maya city who held his position for life, and passed it on to his son—very few women ruled.

bataboob: the nominated local leaders and officials who they were members of the noble class

ppolm: merchant traders.

memba uinicoob: common workers, who made up most of the Maya population.

pentacoob: the Mayan word for slaves, a group that included people in debt, criminals, and war prisoners—many were used for human sacrifices.

as this was the Maya golden age. It was during these years that the Maya reached their greatness as a society. Cities grew strong, and skills and knowledge flourished. Archaeologists have found many ceramic objects, wall paintings, and jewelry items that show the artistic skills of the ancient Maya. Experts have also discovered a handful of Maya books, called codices, which prove that the Maya wrote down every syllable they spoke. This was just one accomplishment that set them apart from their Mesoamerican neighbors.

Another factor that set the Maya apart from their neighbors was their knowledge in the field of mathematics. The ancient Maya developed a counting system based on the number 20. The system used "steps" to increase numbers by multiples of twenty. This allowed the Maya to calculate into the millions. That was handy, because the Maya didn't have computers or calculators! Yet the Maya thought up another mathematical concept that was even more amazing for their time. They were the first people on earth to use zero as a place holder. Not even the Greeks or Romans thought to do that.

Smart ideas, however, couldn't keep Maya cities from collapsing. Around 750 CE, the southern lowland cities failed, one after another. By 1000 CE, many sat empty and abandoned. Archaeologists aren't sure why the Maya left their cities, but they have some ideas. Most experts believe the populations of cities became too great for the amount of

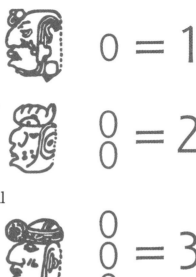

O = 1

O
O = 2

O
O
O = 3

O
O
O
O = 4

| = 5

Hieroglyphs for numbers 1–5 and their symbols.

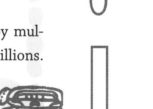

DID YOU KNOW?

Skeletons dating from around 850 CE show that the Maya living in the southern lowlands suffered from starvation and diseases like malaria and yellow fever.

IN 1502, CHRISTOPHER COLUMBUS LEARNED OF THE MAYA WHEN HE CAPTURED A MAYA TRADING CANOE NEAR THE GULF OF HONDURAS. WORD SOON SPREAD IN SPAIN ABOUT THE RICH CULTURES OF MESO-AMERICA, WHICH ATTRACTED SPANISH CONQUISTADORS IN SEARCH OF GOLD. THIS LED TO THE DOWNFALL OF THE AZTEC AND MAYA.

food farmers could produce. Residents left the cities when they began to starve.

Other archaeologists believe common workers left the cities when they got tired of working for their kings. Or maybe the Maya fled their cities because of disease, earthquake, and war. Experts are pretty sure that 95 percent of the ancient Maya living in the southern lowlands died within a relatively short time period. The rest moved to cities in the northern lowlands of

WHO WERE THE AZTEC?

The Aztec came after the decline of the Maya and ruled much of southern and central Mexico in the fifteenth and early sixteenth centuries CE. By 1325 CE, they had completed construction of their huge capital city, Tenochtitlán, built on an island. The city had more than 50,000 residents who lived on corn, beans, chili peppers, squash, tomatoes, and tobacco. The Aztec believed in many gods, including *Coyolxauhqui* (the moon goddess), *Tlaloc* (the rain god), and *Quetzalcoatl* (the god of wind who brings the rains). Like the Maya, the Aztec believed their gods demanded blood sacrifices. To have success in war, the Aztec sacrificed many victims at the same time, carving their still-beating hearts from their chests. The Aztec were known for their gold jewelry, and in 1519, conquistador Hernán Cortés led more than 500 soldiers into Aztec territory in search of gold. At first the Aztec thought Cortés was a god, so they gave him great respect and gold. But they attacked Cortés and his men when they saw their gold being loaded onto ships headed for Spain. In 1521, the Spanish took control of Tenochtitlán, and Aztec society abruptly ended. Today, Mexico City is built over its ruins.

the Yucatán Peninsula. These northern cities remained strong until Spanish soldiers called **conquistadors** invaded the Maya homeland and forced the Maya to be their slaves.

The Spanish sailed to Central America to claim gold for their king, Charles V. One of the first conquistadors to arrive was Hernán Cortés, in 1519. After Cortés took all of the gold from the Aztec, the Spanish looked to see what they could take from the Maya. They didn't find gold, so they took their land instead.

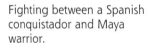

The shadow of Cortés on horseback with the Spanish flag.

When the Spanish soldiers arrived, the ancient Maya were living in 16 large city-states in the northern Yucatán Peninsula, including Chichén Itzá, Uxmal, Tulum, and Mayapán. The Maya fought back when the soldiers attacked, but they were no match for the conquistadors. Why were the Spanish able to conquer the Maya?

First, the Spanish had better weapons. The Maya fought with spears and arrows, but the conquistadors used canons, guns, metal weapons, and horses. The Maya had never seen horses before! Written records mention how surprised the Maya warriors were when the Spanish jumped off their wounded horses to

Fighting between a Spanish conquistador and Maya warrior.

keep fighting. The Maya had assumed the horses and riders were a single being.

Second, the Maya and conquistadors had different war strategies. The Spanish saw war as a way to destroy their enemies and take their goods. The Maya could not understand this level of destruction. The Maya believed that life was sacred, and murder a crime. Even before killing an animal, Maya hunters prayed to it. They thanked it, saying, "I have need." They viewed blood sacrifice the same way—as a necessary part of the life cycle.

WORDS TO KNOW

conquistador: Sixteenth-century Spanish soldiers who conquered and enslaved the Maya.

colonist: A new settler or founder of a colony who is originally from somewhere else.

Third, the Spanish brought new diseases to the Maya, which killed millions of them. These diseases included measles, chicken pox, and smallpox. And finally, Maya priests had predicted that Maya cities would fall before a foreign enemy, and so many of the Maya had simply given up when the Spanish attacked them.

By 1547, the Spanish had managed to make slaves of many Maya, except those who fled deep into the rainforest. The Spanish also tore down many Maya cities so they could build new Spanish cities for their **colonists**, who took the best Maya farmlands. They forced the Maya to grow new crops for Spain, including onions, garlic, wheat, cumin, oregano, cinnamon, rice, olives, limes, bananas, coffee, and sugar cane.

Today, about 6 million Maya live throughout Central America and southern Mexico. Most still do not own their farmland. As a people they have shown incredible strength and character in facing all of the challenges that have been thrust upon them in the modern world.

CHAPTER 2

KINGS

Unlike their Aztec neighbors, the ancient Maya people were not ruled by one king. Each Maya city had its own king. The ancient Maya called these kings *halch uinic,* which means "true man."

Some ancient Maya cities remained small, but others grew and combined to form large city-states. This happened when kings captured enemy kings, or when royal families in different cities were united through marriage. Some city-states had more than 50,000 residents. That's a lot of people to feed!

City residents worked hard to help keep their cities strong and running smoothly, and they did so without complaint. Why? Because Maya commoners believed in putting their king and city first. It was the king's job to bring good fortune to the city. The Maya respected their kings because they believed they spoke directly to the **gods**. The common people believed that they could ask the gods for favors during their daily offerings, but that the gods liked the king best. In return for the king asking the gods to bless their city, workers worked hard for the king. If crops failed, however, or disease ripped through the city, the Maya believed the gods were punishing them—or their kings. This was a good time for rival kings to attack.

A Maya king.

The Maya punished anyone who didn't obey and serve the king by enslaving or killing them. Slaves were the lowest class in society and had to do whatever they were told. There were three ways in which the ancient Maya became slaves: they were captured by a rival city during a war raid, they were sold by their family to pay off a debt, or they were caught stealing. The Maya believed that stealing was so wrong that they killed any thief who stole a second time. The Maya did this to rid the city of the thief's evil spirit.

Slaves were highly valued by the royals—and not only because the slaves did so much work. Slaves were

DID YOU KNOW?

If you were to visit a Maya city in a time machine, it would be easy to tell who the slaves were. They had really short haircuts, and their bodies were often painted in black and white stripes.

A stone stela of 18 Rabbit, the king who ruled Copán for over 40 years until he was captured and sacrificed by a rival also valuable because they made for good **sacrifices** to the gods! Sometimes priests and royals bought slaves from trade merchants for this very purpose.

Maya artists often painted pictures of kings sitting on their thrones. These kings usually had at least one bodyguard hovering nearby, to protect them against surprise war raids. Maya kings feared being captured, tortured, and beheaded by a rival king as part of a blood sacrifice. One famous Maya king who met this fate was Waxaklajuun Ub'aah K'awiil, whose name translates to "18 Rabbit." From about 695 to 738 CE, 18 Rabbit ruled the city of Copán. His head was chopped off by Cauac Sky, the king of a rival city-state.

Warriors usually attacked rival cities at night, suddenly announcing their presence with a loud horn blare. The warriors dressed in tall **headdresses** and animal **pelts**. In their hands they carried flint-tipped wooden spears and shields woven from the palm strips of

WORDS TO KNOW

gods: A superhuman being that is worshipped.

sacrifice: An offering to a god.

headdress: An elaborate covering for the head worn during ceremonial occasions.

pelt: An animal skin.

quetzal: A bird prized by Maya kings for its brilliant blue-green feathers. Today this bird faces extinction.

cacao: A rainforest tree that produces a cacao bean. Maya kings loved the bitter chocolate drink from these beans.

DID YOU KNOW?

With so many residents to feed, kings often fought over croplands. But war raids were also held to steal people for slavery and human sacrifices.

DEATH & BURIAL

Though death was a common part of their lives, the ancient Maya feared their own deaths. They considered an "ordinary" death to be the worst way to die. Why? Because they believed that dying from disease or old age meant being doomed to an eternity in the cold and unhappy underworld. The honor of living in paradise, they believed, was only guaranteed to warriors who died in battle, to women who died in childbirth, and to sacrificial victims.

A carved scene from Yaxchilán showing warriors taking captives.

palm trees, or animal skins. And their wives traveled with them! War raids lasted several weeks at most. They were never held when it was time to plant or harvest crops, as this source of food was critical to all of the city-states.

When commoners died, they were buried beneath the floor of their simple mud houses. Buried with them were the personal items they had used in life, and a jadeite bead was placed in their mouths to prepare them for re-birth in the next world.

Kings got a much more elaborate send off. They were buried in majestic tombs, with enough clothing, weapons, and slaves to serve them in the afterlife. Even

THE MAYA USED CACAO BEANS AS MONEY. SOME TRADERS TRIED TO FOOL BUYERS WITH FAKE BEANS. THESE DISHONEST MEN FILLED EMPTY BEAN PODS WITH SAND. EVERYONE SOON LEARNED TO TEST THE BEANS TO MAKE SURE THEY WERE SOLID BY BITING THEM.

Cacao pods.

Cacao beans.

THE MAYA INVENTED CHOCOLATE DRINKS!

The Maya farmed cacao trees just so the kings could have their favorite frothy chocolate drinks whenever they wanted. Cacao trees grow in the damp shade of Central American rainforests. They don't bear fruit until they are 4 or 5 years old. Then, each tree sprouts flower blossoms that must be fertilized by tiny gnats before they become seed pods. The Maya dried the beans, ground them up, and mixed them with water. Then they poured it from one drinking jar to another to make it foamy. When Spanish soldiers arrived, they grew to love the taste of cacao. But they added sugar to their chocolate drinks to make them less bitter. They shipped the beans back to Spain and the Spanish royal families fell in love with the drink, too. Today, factory workers harvest the cacao pods. They split each hard pod open with a heavy wooden hammer and remove the 40 or so beans, which are surrounded by sticky, white pulp. Beans are dried in the sun, and then roasted at a high temperature to bring out their flavor. A special machine separates the shell of the bean from the inside of the bean, which is called the nib. The nibs are ground until they turn into a thick paste. This paste is used to make your favorite candy bars!

favorite dogs were buried with them! Before their bodies were sealed in tombs, the kings were adorned in pieces of jadeite jewelry. Pacal II, the great king of Palenque, was buried with a jadeite burial mask that covered his entire face. This piece shows the great skill of ancient Maya artists.

Kings faced stress and danger, but they also enjoyed many perks. They got to dress in jaguar pelts, fancy jewelry, and the beautiful tail

DID YOU KNOW?

Written records found by archaeologists tell us that an adult male slave could be bought with one hundred cacao beans.

feathers of the **quetzal** bird. They got to live with their families and advisors in beautiful stone palaces. And they got to drink lots of frothy chocolate drinks made from **cacao** (pronounced ka-KOW) seeds. The royals liked this drink so much that cacao became the currency of the Maya, like money. The common workers couldn't drink it because they couldn't afford it.

Maya glyphs for quetzal (*top*) and cacao (*bottom*).

A quetzal bird.

Make Your Own
MEXICAN HOT CHOCOLATE

1 Have your parents help you warm the milk and chocolate in a saucepan over low heat. Use a whisk to mix the melted chocolate into the steaming milk. Remove the hot mixture from the stovetop.

2 To froth the milk, stir hard with the whisk. Or, you can do what the Maya did to froth their chocolate drink: pour the milk from one cup to another until it fills with air bubbles. Serve it in two cups.

SUPPLIES

saucepan

whisk

2 cups milk

4-ounce-disk pressed dark bitter Mexican chocolate (a popular brand is "Ibarra")

2 drinking cups

Make Your Own
ROYAL "JADEITE" BURIAL MASK

1 Place the plastic face mask face up on your wax paper or newspaper. If you are using a milk jug, cut the jug in half at the seam with the Xacto knife or sharp scissors. You can use either side to make a mask, but the handle makes a good nose shape.

2 Lay sheets of the tissue paper on top of each other and cut or tear the stack into strips and then a variety of shapes. Each piece becomes a "jadeite" tile. Set these to the side where you can easily reach them. If you are using magazine pages for your jadeite tiles, select as many different shades of green as you can find.

3 **If using glue:** Use your foam brush to add a thin layer of glue to a small section of your mask. Cover the glue with your paper tiles. Continue this process until the entire mask is covered in several layers of "jadeite."

SUPPLIES

wax paper or newspaper

3-D craft plastic face mask (full-face craft masks are sold in craft stores) OR gallon-size milk jug

Xacto knife OR scissors

green tissue paper OR green-colored pages from old magazines

bottle of decoupage solution (with brush) OR watered-down Elmer's white glue and foam brush

black and white paint

paint brush

4 **If using decoupage solution:** Use the brush included in the bottle to cover a small section of the mask. Cover with the paper tiles. When done, brush a final coat of the decoupage solution over the finished mask. This will give it a hard finish. Allow the mask to dry overnight.

5 Paint white ovals to make eye sockets for the face. When the white paint is dry, paint round black circles on the ovals for the eyeballs.

CHAPTER 3

PRIESTS AND HEALERS

Like the kings, **priests** were highly respected by city residents. Many priests were members of royal families. It was their job to communicate with the gods and make important decisions about when crops should be planted, when women should have babies, and when special religious ceremonies should be held. They made these predictions by studying the movements of the planets, moon, and stars. They were helped by **scribes**, who wrote down their calculations.

Clay figurine of a priest with gods protruding from serpents' mouths in his headdress.

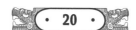

Shaman-priests were skilled doctors. They were different from regular priests in that they took care of the physical needs of the people. They made medicinal potions from animal dung, urine, crocodile and rooster testicles, bat wings, and live toads. Yuck! But they also prescribed steam baths and used herbs, such as leaves and juice from the agave plant, to brew healing teas. Today, medical researchers are studying ancient Maya remedies. They hope what they learn will help doctors to treat sick people around the world today.

When seeing a sick patient, the first thing the shaman-priest did was try to sort out the cause of the illness. They did this by "reading" animal bones that they threw on the ground.

A figurine of a shaman.

WORDS TO KNOW

priest: A person with special religious status who performed sacrifices and rituals, and took care of the spiritual needs of society.

scribe: A member of Maya society who wrote with hieroglyphs on many types of surfaces, as well as in codices, to keep records of all kinds.

shaman-priest: A priest-doctor in Maya society who tended to the physical needs of the people. The shaman-priest used magic, sorcery, and medicines made from plants and the natural world, for healing, divination, and control over natural events.

loincloth: A strip of cloth worn around the mid-section of the body.

A drawing of a typical priest from Chichén Itzá.

Shaman-priests offered sacrifices to gods they thought might be angry. Sometimes they even bled the body part that hurt the patient, to get rid of any evil spirits. So if someone suffered from headaches, the shaman-priests might make cuts in their forehead. Aren't you glad you can take aspirin instead?!

Shaman-priests were more than just healers. They blessed ceremonies that were important in the daily lives of the ancient Maya, like the coming-of-age ceremonies of Maya boys and girls. These were held to publicly announce that the boys and girls were no longer children. Another ceremony was marriage. Official matchmakers, called *atanzahob*, assisted the shaman-priests in arranging marriages. It was their job to check that the stars predicted good fortune for the bride and groom. The *atanzahob* also made sure that a groom paid a fair price for his bride.

Wedding ceremonies took place at the home of the bride's family. The mother of the groom embroidered a special marriage **loincloth** for her son. She also stitched a special blouse for her new daughter-in-law. She may have used a diamond pattern, as it represented the earth and sky. To celebrate the happy day, guests were treated to a wonderful feast. They ate turkey *tamales* (steamed cornmeal dumplings), beans, and tortillas.

Shaman priest.

A diamond pattern.

Mayan glyphs for woman (*top*) and spouse (*bottom*).

NEWLY MARRIED COUPLES MADE A NEW NAME BY JOINING THEIR NAMES. WHEN THEY HAD FAMILIES OF THEIR OWN, EACH OF THEIR CHILDREN TOOK A *NAAL*, OR "HOUSE NAME," FROM THEIR MOTHER. THIS NAME COULD ONLY BE PASSED THROUGH THE FEMALE SIDE OF THE FAMILY. MAYA CHILDREN ALSO TOOK THEIR FATHER'S NAME, WHICH WAS THE NAME THEY WERE CALLED EVERY DAY.

After the wedding feast, the groom moved in with his wife's family for 5 to 7 years. After that the couple moved permanently into or nearby the home of the groom's family. The Maya believed in ending unhappy marriages. A marriage was considered over when a couple decided to separate. If either person wanted to remarry after the divorce, they simply chose a new partner. For a second marriage, they skipped the matchmaker and wedding ceremony. Kings often had more than one wife, but common people could only have one spouse at a time.

MAYA UNIVERSE

The Maya believed the universe was divided into three layers. The upper layer contained the stars and was the home of the sky kings. The middle layer was the earth. The lower level was the underworld or *Xibalba*, which translates to "place of awe." This was the home of evil gods. The center of the earth, from which the world tree sprouted, was green. The Maya called this tree *wakah-chan*, which means "raised-up sky." Its branches supported the sky, but its roots burrowed deep into the underworld.

Mayan glyph for *Xibalba*.

The Maya believed the earth was flat with four corners. They also believed that four jaguars of different colors held up the four corners of the sky. The jaguar in the east was red, the jaguar in the north was white, the jaguar in the west was black, and the jaguar in the south was yellow. According to the Maya, the Jaguar god inhabited the underworld, home of the dead, but each morning he became the Sun god, who traveled across the sky from east to west, then returned to the underworld every evening.

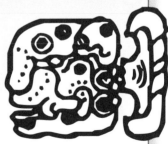
Mayan glyph for the Jaguar god of the underworld.

Make Your Own

3-D FOUR CORNERS OF THE EARTH COMPASS

1 Trace two copies of the tree template onto one of the sheets of green paper, or trace it onto white paper and then color it in with green marker. Cut out the trees.

2 Fit the two tree pieces together by cutting where the dotted lines are shown on the template (a slit in the bottom center of one piece, a slit in the top center of the other). This allows your tree to stand up by itself.

3 Trace four copies of the jaguar templates. You need one each in red, black, yellow, and white. Use colored paper or color the white jaguars with markers. Notice that there are two parts to the template. One part is the jaguar's body, the other is the jaguar's legs. You will need to trace and cut out the leg templates twice for each color, once for the front and once for the back legs.

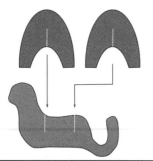

4 Fit the jaguar pieces together by cutting where the dotted lines are shown on the template (two slits in the top of the jaguar's body and a slit in the bottom center of each leg piece).

5 Position the tree in the middle of the second green piece of construction paper or cardstock. Write the letters N, S, E, and W between the trunk legs in black marker. These stand for the compass directions north, south, east, and west.

6 Position a jaguar in each corner. Make sure you get the colors right: east is red, north is white, west is black, and south is yellow.

7 If you want to keep the tree and jaguars in place, apply a coat of glue to the bottom edge of each and press gently onto the green "earth."

8 If you want to make it look like clouds are passing over the tree, pull the cotton balls apart until they are light and wispy. Drape them over the branches of the tree.

SUPPLIES

6 pieces of heavy white construction paper or cardstock, 8½ by 11 inches (or 2 pieces of green and 1 each of red, black, yellow, and white)

pencil

jaguar and tree templates included on next page

markers (red, green, yellow, and black if you are using white paper)

scissors

glue

1 or 2 cotton balls (optional)

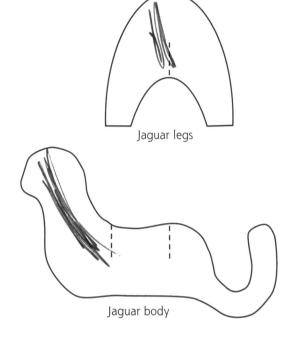

Jaguar legs

Jaguar body

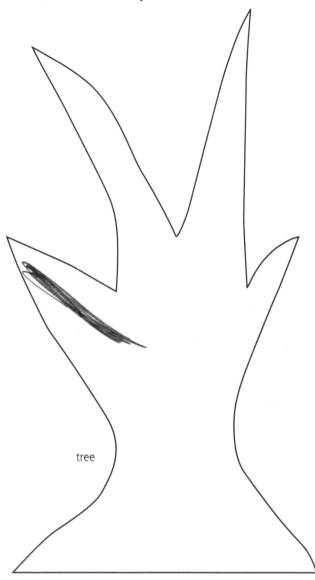

tree

red jaguar

yellow jaguar

white jaguar

black jaguar

Overhead view of compass. Jaguars go in each corner and the tree is in the middle.

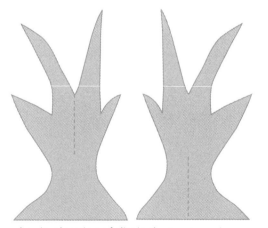

showing location of slits in the two tree pieces

MERCHANTS

Like kings and priests, trade **merchants** also played a critical role in society. They saw to it that food and other items were bought and sold all over Mesoamerica. Merchants from the lowlands, for example, traveled to other cities to sell honey, cotton cloth, tobacco, vanilla, cacao beans, and animal skins. **Jadeite**, obsidian, **copal**, and the quetzal feathers worn only by kings came from the highlands. Merchants from the coastal cities sold dried fish, turtle eggs, shells, pearls, and salt. All of these merchants preferred to peddle their goods in the busy city squares.

A merchant with porters transporting goods for trade. Note the tumplines around the porters' foreheads.

THE QUETZAL BIRD

The quetzal bird is a member of the trogon bird family, and it is similar to the road runner. They nest in trees and holes throughout the jungle, and they have striking bronze-green feathers. Because these feathers were so beautiful, and the quetzal bird was considered to be sacred, only kings were allowed to wear them.

WORDS TO KNOW

merchant: A buyer and seller of different items for profit.

jadeite: A rare and prized mineral, usually emerald to light green, used by the Maya to make jewelry.

copal: A kind of sap that comes from tropical trees that is used in candles.

Often, the merchants traveled long distances to trade with the Toltec and Aztec, their Mexican neighbors in the west. On land they carried their goods on their backs, as they didn't have horses or other pack animals. They also carried goods in a sling called a tumpline. This sling hung from a strap across the forehead. It is possible for people to carry loads weighing as much as 70 percent of their body weight with a tumpline. That means that a man who weighs 150 pounds could carry over 100 pounds using a tumpline. Maya traders even crossed rivers and the ocean to reach the Caribbean and Panama. To do so, they used large wooden canoes called *chem*. The Maya carved *chem* from the trunks of mahogany and other hardwood trees. At more than 40 feet long, the canoes were so large they could carry 20 people!

Some experts believe the ancient Maya may have played a game of chance called *Bul*. In the Mayan language, the word *bul* means "dice." But *bul* was also a game of war: the goal of the game was to

Playing *bul*.

"kill" your opponent. This game was played by adults and children, probably more so by the wealthy, like merchants, who had servants and more time for leisure activity. Though we're not exactly sure how the ancient Maya played the game, it is possible that they played it as the Maya living in Guatemala do today.

PLAY BUL!

1 To start the game, you'll need to make your "game board." Simply place 15 kernels of corn in a straight line, each about 2 inches apart, horizontally between you and your opponent. As you play, you will move your 5 game pieces in the spaces between the corn kernels.

2 Make your "dice" from four pieces of flat-sided corn. Use the marker to draw a dot on one side of each kernel. When you throw the kernels, you get a point for every dot that faces up when the kernels land. If four blank sides face up, you get five points!

3 You also need to make your 5 game pieces. The ancient Maya may have used pieces of cotton, sticks, or stones. You can make yours from clay, but make sure each piece is about the same shape and size and that they can sit atop one another (for this reason flat disc shapes are ideal). If your game pieces are all the same color, paint one set a different color so you can tell yours apart from your opponent's.

4 Now you just need to know the rules in order to play:

❂ Each player places their game pieces at the end of the game board that is to their right. Players sit facing each other, so each moves along the board from their right to their left.

❂ The player to go first is the one who gets the highest number of points throwing the four pieces of corn.

❂ The player to start throws the corn again, then moves a game piece the correct number of spaces. One point

means a game piece moves to the first space from his or her end of the game board.

❂ The second player then throws the corn and enters the board from his or her end, so that the opposing game pieces are moving toward each other.

❂ On the second roll, players can either move the first game piece farther down the row, or add a second game piece to the board.

❂ You cannot place two of your own pieces on the same space, but you can land on a space occupied by your opponent! When this happens, cover your opponent's piece with your piece. On the next throw, move the pieces together toward the end of the board.

❂ If you are able to get this game piece all the way to the end of the board without being landed on by your opponent, you get to keep your opponent's piece and put your piece back on the board by reentering it from the right side.

❂ The game gets really exciting if your opponent lands on a piece of yours that is holding one of his or her pieces hostage! When this happens, your opponent's piece sits atop the stack (which is now three levels high), and it now must be moved toward your opponent's end of the board (to his or her left). If your opponent is able to reach the end of the board without you intercepting the piece, his or her pieces can reenter the game board from the right side, and your piece is out of the game. How's that for reversal of fortune?

The game ends when one player loses all their pieces.

SUPPLIES

19 kernels of dried corn

flat playing surface (floor or tabletop)

magic markers

5 game pieces for each player, like coins or flat clay disks

CHAPTER 5

FARMING AND FOOD

The **commoners** (*memba uinicoob*) of Maya societies enjoyed few luxuries in life. They lived in simple mud houses and worked hard all day long. Unless they were on a war raid, the men were either planting and harvesting crops or building pyramids and roadways. The main crop of the Maya was maize, what we call corn. Farmers also grew black and red beans, squash, pumpkins, chili peppers, tomatoes, avocados, papayas, and sweet potatoes.

Maya commoners went to bed early as a family, sleeping together in the same room. In the morning they rose early, so the men could get to the fields before the

CORN WAS A SPIRITUAL CROP TO THE MAYA, AS IT SYMBOLIZED BIRTH AND DEATH. THE MAYA EVEN WORSHIPPED *YUM-KAAX*, THE GOD OF CORN. SINCE CORN WAS SO IMPORTANT TO THE MAYA, THE SUCCESS OR FAILURE OF THE CORN CROP COULD BE THE DIFFERENCE BETWEEN LIFE AND DEATH. *YUM-KAAX* WAS A FRIENDLY AND GENEROUS GOD.

Yum-Kaax, the god of corn.

day got really hot. Farmers used pointed sticks to dig holes in the ground for their crop seeds. They did not have horses to help them plow the fields, nor did they have metal tools or the machines we have today. This made farming difficult, slow work. Maya farmers often worked in groups so they could harvest more crops during the growing season.

During the Maya classic period (250–900 CE), farmers developed some smart ways of farming. In low swamp areas, for example, they built raised fields. They tucked flat **terraces** into hillsides to prevent the soil from washing away during rains. And they **rotated** their crops every couple of years so the soil had time to rest between plantings.

In areas without rivers, the ancient Maya did something really inventive: they dug **reservoirs**. A reservoir is like a giant bowl that collects rainwater. An ancient Maya reservoir can be found in the ruins of Tikal, a city in northern Guatemala. Tikal is also surrounded by 10 reservoirs, each of which held up to 40 million gallons of water! In places where they had too much water, the Maya built canals and **aqueducts** to channel

A modern-day agave farm in Mexico. The ancient Maya used the sisal fibers of the agave plant to make rope.

DID YOU KNOW?

The Maya created chewing gum, which they called *cha*. They took the thick, milky sap that oozed out of the wild sapodilla tree, waited until it hardened, and then chewed it.

FROM FUNGUS TO FOOD

Many people in Mexico today make corn dishes with *huitlacoche* (pronounced wheat-lah-KOH-chay). It's a fungus that grows in sweet corn, making the kernels turn grey or black as they fill with spores that share the consistency of mushrooms and taste sweet, savory, and earthy. For a time, American corn farmers called this disease "corn smut" and fed it to their pigs. Recently, however, the best chefs at fancy restaurants in America have been serving it to their customers, and it has become a delicacy.

WORDS TO KNOW

commoners: Most of the people in Maya society. Commoners were those who were not kings, other royalty, priests, merchants, government officials, or the wealthy.

terraces: Level areas cut into a steep slope to provide a flat section for crops.

crop rotation: Growing a different crop each year on the same piece of land, and letting a piece of land rest every few years.

reservoir: A natural or artificial pond or lake used to store and regulate the supply of water.

aqueduct: A pipe or channel designed to transport water from one place to another—water flows through the aqueduct by force of gravity.

drought: A period of little or no rain that causes extensive damage to crops or prevents them from growing at all.

hearth: The floor of a fire or oven.

gnarled: Twisted and deformed.

water through the cities. You'll see an old aqueduct if you visit the ruins of Palenque.

As creative and successful as the Maya farmers were when it came to collecting and channeling water to their crops, during **drought** periods their reservoirs and aqueducts were sometimes in danger of drying out. During these periods, it is believed that the Maya would make rain sticks to encourage the rain to fall from the sky and give their crops a drink. Rain sticks are musical instruments. They are hollow tubes with pins stuck through them, filled at one end with small beads or beans. When one side of the stick is upended, the beads inside fall to the other end of the tube, and as they bounce off the pins, they sound a lot like a rainstorm.

The Maya ate corn tortillas at every meal. Corn had to be ground fresh every day, because it didn't keep well

A rain stick.

MAKING TORTILLAS IS HARD WORK!

The Maya did not use forks or spoons like we do. They used tortillas! Rolled up, the tortillas worked like spoons for sauces and beans. It took a lot of tortillas to feed everyone in the family this way—and a lot of effort to turn dried corn into flat tortillas. Every night, women set dried corn kernels to soak in a pot of water and lime to soften them. At around four in the morning, the women got up to grind the softened corn into flour and make dough. Then they were ready to make their tortillas. After building fires under their three-stone **hearths**, Maya women patted the dough into patties and baked the day's tortillas one at a time.

in the humid climate. They used a tool called a metate: a slab of rock about one foot wide and one and a half feet long. With it they used a stone tool called a *metlapil*. It looks like the rolling pins we use today to roll out pie crust. Women crushed corn into fine flour by rolling the *metlapil* over the corn kernels. They then mixed the flour with water to make dough. Experts know that Maya women spent a lot of time on their knees grinding corn because the knee bones of Maya women's skeletons that have been discovered over the years are gnarled. Knee bones of the skeletons of royal women, however, are not **gnarled** because they had slaves to do the work.

DID YOU KNOW?

The Maya believed that flint produced sparks because it contained the spirit of lightning.

Another tool for grinding, called a mortar and pestle.

Make Your Own
HOMEMADE TORTILLAS

In the photo to the left, a mother grinds maize with stone tools as the elder daughter pats the dough into tortillas. You can make tortillas too!

1 Mix the ingredients with a wooden spoon to form a dough. On a lightly floured surface, knead the dough until it is no longer sticky. This will take about 5 minutes.

2 Put the dough in a glass bowl and cover it with plastic wrap. Let the covered bowl sit on the counter for about an hour.

3 Divide the dough into 12 equal pieces. Remove one piece at a time from the covered bowl, as the plastic wrap will keep the remaining dough from drying out.

4 Roll the piece of dough into a ball with your hands and then flatten it between your palms. Use your fingertips to stretch the dough into a thin circle. You can also roll the dough with a rolling pin between two pieces of plastic wrap if that helps you to evenly thin it out.

5 When your dough is nice and flat, get your parents to help you fry them in the skillet at medium-high heat. Flip the frying tortilla to brown both sides. Keep them warm wrapped in tin foil.

6 Hot tortillas are really good with butter but you can try them with many other different fillings, like shredded cheese and salsa. Roll them up and enjoy!

SUPPLIES

2 cups masa harina (corn flour)

1 cup warm chicken broth

½ teaspoon salt

mixing bowl

wooden spoon

glass bowl

plastic wrap

rolling pin

frying pan or cast iron skillet regular

tin foil

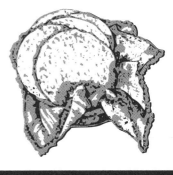

Make Your Own
CORNHUSK
HAT

The climate of Mesoamerica is very hot. Given the powerful sunlight, the Maya farmers may have worn cornhusk hats like these.

1 If you are using dried cornhusks, you'll need to soak them in water for 5 to 10 minutes to soften them. Use a large bowl or your kitchen sink. Pat the husks with paper towels to dry them off. They will be damp. If you are using newspaper or paper towels to make your hat, cut or tear strips about 2 inches wide and 10 inches long. Trim the ends so that one end is slightly narrower than the other.

2 Separate one husk from the pile and lay it on the table so the narrow tip is pointed away from you. Run a thin line of glue down one long side of the husk. Overlap it with a second husk, making sure that the pointed ends (the ones away from you) are touching. Press the husks together, setting the glue. You can staple the husks together instead if you prefer.

3 Continue to overlap the husks until you have made a circle, with the pointed ends in the center of the circle.

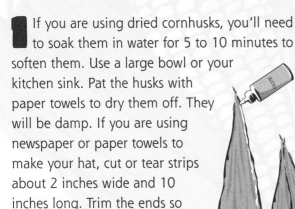

4 Grasp the pointed ends and stand the hat upright. About an inch from the top, use the raffia or string to tie the pointed ends of the husks together.

5 Settle the hat over your overturned medium bowl. Braid several long pieces of raffia and then glue the braids around the hat for decoration.

6 Place the smaller bowl on top of the medium bowl. This "mold" will ensure your hat dries in the right shape.

7 Remove the small bowl and trim the ends of the cornhusks so that they are even. Your hat is now ready to wear!

SUPPLIES

dried or fresh cornhusks or strips of paper towel or newspaper at least 10 inches long (you may need 20 or more per hat)*

paper towels

scissors

hot glue gun, glue stick, or stapler

raffia or string*

medium-sized bowl about the size of your head

smaller bowl

* Cornhusks can be found at a grocery or craft store, or saved in late summer from corn on the cob. Raffia is available in craft stores.

Make Your Own
RAIN STICK

Rain sticks are fun to make and fun to play with. They make a beautiful sound.

1 Use a fine-tipped black marker or pen to draw dots about a half inch apart all the way down the spiral seam of the cardboard tube.

2 Poke a 1-inch nail all the way in at each dot.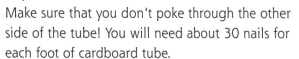
Make sure that you don't poke through the other side of the tube! You will need about 30 nails for each foot of cardboard tube.

3 After you have finished poking in all the nails, carefully wrap the tape all the way around the tube to hold the nails in place.

4 Cut two circles of paper just a little bigger than the ends of the tube. Put one of the paper circles over one end of the tube using a rubber band. Cover the circle and rubber band with tape so the whole end of the tube is sealed shut.

5 Put a handful of rice or beans into the open end of the tube. You can cover the open end with your hand, and turn the tube over to hear the sound of your rain stick. Add or remove rice or beans until you like the sound. Beans will make a louder sound while rice will make a softer sound.

6 Place the second circle of paper over the open end of the tube, secure it with a rubber band, and seal that end with tape. Decorate your rain stick however you like.

7 Turn your rain stick over again and again, shake it, and tap it. Enjoy the sound!

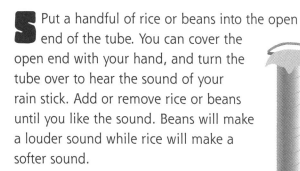

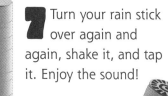

SUPPLIES

cardboard tube (an empty paper towel roll works well, but wrapping paper tube is even better!)

fine-point black marker or pen

60 or more 1-inch nails

heavy-duty tape (masking, packing, or duct tape)

construction paper

scissors

rubber bands

rice or small, uncooked beans

paint, markers, other decorations

CHAPTER 6

WOMEN AND WEAVING

While men were busy in the fields, women worked hard at home. They tended their home gardens and beehives, took care of children, prepared all the family meals, and wove cloth. The looms used by ancient Maya women were called backstrap looms because while one end was tied around a tree, the other end was tied around the weaver's back.

Backstrap looms were small, and they could be very easily carried around and used wherever there was a tree or a post. Ancient Maya codices, as well as painted or carved stelae and glyphs show images of Maya women using backstrap looms. Two thousand years later, the Maya still view

A spindle whorl.

the backstrap loom as a sacred symbol and they still use it to weave cloth.

To make thread from their cotton crops, Maya weavers used a tool called a **spindle whorl**. As they twirled a foot-long stick, weighted and balanced by a disk near its bottom, they fed cotton fibers to the stick with their other hand. As the cotton twisted, thread was made. From there, the weavers colored the thread with vegetable and mineral dyes, and then wove cloth using a hand or backstrap loom. Commoners wore very simple clothing: men wore a loincloth called an *ex* and women wore loose, embroidered dresses called *huipils* and a light shawl called a *pati*.

In addition to cloth for royalty, weavers made everyday items, such as baskets, sleeping mats, fans, hats, and shoes. These were made from rainforest palm trees and **sisal** fibers from the **agave** (pronounced ah-GAH-vay) plant. The agave is a cactus plant with needle-sharp spines. Its leaves can grow as long as 6 feet! When the pulp of these leaves is removed by pounding or pressing, tough strands of sisal fibers remain.

A backstrap loom.

A Maya woman in traditional clothing.

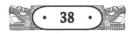

Ornamental pattern produced by wrapping dark fibers with lighter ones before weaving.

An ancient clay figurine of a Maya woman weaving.

The agave plant depends on a specific type of moth to pollinate it. This moth is very important because if it doesn't stuff pollen balls into the cup-shaped stigma of each flower, the plants can't reproduce. But what's really interesting is that the moth is just as dependent on the plant. Without agave seeds to eat, the moth caterpillars would starve after hatching! Fortunately for the ancient Maya, the agave flourished, enabling them to make cords, baskets, and sandals from the long, strong fibers.

An agave plant.

WORDS TO KNOW

spindle whorl: A rod or pin, tapered at one end and usually weighted at the other, on which fibers are spun into thread and then wound.

sisal: Stiff fibers from the agave leaves used by the Maya to make rope and many other things.

agave: A type of cactus plant that grows in Central America. The Maya used it for its sisal fibers.

Make Your Own
LOOM AND CLOTH

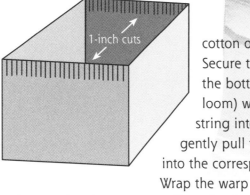
1-inch cuts

1 Cut the top (or flaps) off of a cardboard box. Using your ruler and a pencil, mark every quarter inch or every eighth inch on two opposite sides of the cardboard box. Make sure that the marks on one side line up with the marks on the other side. Then make 1-inch cuts on each of the marks you measured.

2 Next you need to string your warp, or the lengthwise strings of the weaving. Use a sturdy

cotton or linen yarn for the warp. Secure the end of the warp thread to the bottom of your cardboard box (or loom) with a piece of tape. Slide the string into the first slit on one side and gently pull the string across the loom and into the corresponding slit on the other side. Wrap the warp thread around the bottom, pulling the thread into the next slit on the other side of the box edge. Continue to wrap the warp around the box until all slits are full. Tighten any loose threads to an even tension, and then secure the other end of the warp string on the bottom with a piece of tape.

3 Now your loom is ready for weaving. Choose the yarn you want to start with and tie one end of the yarn to the first warp string and wrap the other end of the yarn around your pencil. Put a

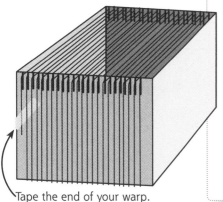
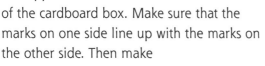
Tape the end of your warp.

piece of tape around the pencil to secure the yarn.

4 Push the pencil under one end and over the next warp thread all the way across until you have woven all the strings and come to the other side. Begin the second row by weaving back toward the direction you just came from. Note that you must weave the second row the opposite way from the first row, going over the warp threads that you just went under, and under the warp threads you just went over. Each row needs to be woven opposite from the row before.

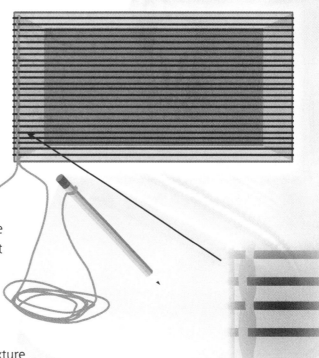

5 If you wish to change the color or texture of the yarn as you are weaving, simply tie one end of the new yarn to the end of the old yarn, and the other end of the new yarn to the end of the pencil. Make sure the knot is pushed to the back of the weaving. Try to periodically pull all the yarn gently to make sure that the fabric is tight and even. Just be careful not to pull it too tightly or your fabric will not have straight edges.

6 When you have woven your fabric and completely filled up the loom, you can finish off your cloth by tying the yarn to the very last warp string. Then cut all warp threads from your cardboard loom and tie pairs of strings on each side together in a tight knot.

A close-up view of the under and over technique used in weaving.

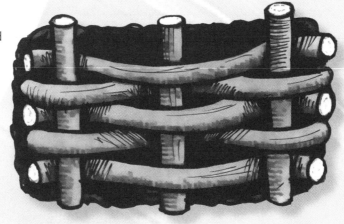

Make Your Own
MAYA SPINDLE WHORL

1 Using a ruler, mark 9 inches from the end of your wooden dowel. Carefully saw through the dowel at that line with the serrated knife. Ask an adult to help you.

2 Push the 9-inch length of dowel through the hole in the wheel far enough so there is 2 inches of the dowel below the wheel.

3 Sharpen each end of the dowel into a point. You can do this with your knife, but the easiest way is to use an electric pencil sharpener!

4 Sit on the floor with your legs crossed like the ancient Maya, and prepare to spin your first cotton thread! You can stand the whorl in a small bowl to help keep it in place when you spin it like a top. Moisten the pointed top of your spindle whirl with your tongue. Hold your spindle whorl in your right hand

and the cotton in your left hand. Poke the top of the whorl into the edge of the cotton, spinning the whorl to the right (clockwise) until some of cotton fibers catch.

5 As you spin the whorl with your right hand, it should be at a slight bend to the left, close to a 45-degree angle. Use your left hand to gently pull the cotton fibers up and away from the spindle tip. Cotton fibers are very short, so don't pull on the cotton too hard or the fibers will pull apart completely. The easiest way to hold the cotton ball is between your first two fingers. Then use your thumb and third finger to smooth the thread.

6 When you've managed to spin about 10 inches of thin thread, wind the thread around the shaft of the whorl just above the wheel. Continue to wind the thread up the shaft until you've used up the cotton ball.

7 This might seem difficult at first, but if you keep practicing you'll quickly get the hang of it! If you want, once you have three or four pieces of yarn, you can dye them and braid them together to make a bracelet.

SUPPLIES

wooden model car wheel, about 2 or 3 inches in diameter (available at most craft stores)

wooden dowel that will fit snugly into the wheel's center hole

ruler

pencil

serrated knife

cotton inserts from aspirin jars OR bundle or raw cotton from a yarn store

CHAPTER 7

MAYA CHILDREN

When boys were around 3 years old, their mothers tied a white bead in their hair to show their purity. When boys reached puberty, around 14 years of age, the bead was removed by a shaman-priest. This ceremony was called the Descent of the Gods. The boy then moved into a house with other young boys until his father decided it was time for him to marry. This usually happened when he was between 18 and 20 years of age. Before marriage, young men painted their bodies and faces black. After marriage, they painted their bodies red.

The ceremony for young Maya girls also involved the removal of a special item. When girls were

THE MAYA HAD DOGS AS PETS JUST LIKE WE DO. THEIR DOGS WERE HAIRLESS, AND COULD SWEAT THROUGH THEIR SKIN. THIS IS UNUSUAL FOR DOGS, BECAUSE MOST CAN ONLY COOL THEMSELVES BY PANTING.

Maya symbol for dog.

small, their mothers tied a tiny red shell around their waists with a string. When they reached 12 years of age, the shell was removed. Girls were usually married by the time they were 14 years old. Until they were married, however, girls could not look men in the eye. If a girl met a man along a path, she stepped aside and turned her back until he passed.

Experts are not entirely sure what Maya children did throughout the day, but they do know that it depended on the status of their families. The children of royalty and upper society probably had more time to play, whereas the children of commoners, farmers and builders probably had to help out in the fields or with chores. Archaeologists have found some ancient Maya children's toys, including a jaguar figure made of clay.

An important family festival that is still celebrated today has roots in Maya history. According to legend the spirits of the

A child's jaguar pull-toy made of clay.

ATOLE

Atole is a traditional hot drink from Mesoamerica made from corn. In Mexico today, it is most commonly drunk on the Day of the Dead, a day for celebrating the lives of dead ancestors.

MAYA VERSION OF HALLOWEEN

Today, the Day of the Dead is most popular in Mexico, where it is a national holiday. Although the topic of this holiday is death, it continues to be a joyful celebration, honoring the lives of deceased ancestors. According to today's version of the holiday, the souls of dead children return on November 1, and the adult spirits follow on November 2. So, between October 31 and November 2, Mexican families clean the gravestones of their loved ones before loading them with sweets, food, and toys. In some towns, families even spend the night in graveyards and bring pillows and blankets for their dead ancestors to rest in after their long journey back to earth from the underworld. Sugar cookies, sugar skulls, and beverages such as atole are popular during this holiday. In some parts of the country, children in costumes roam the streets, asking passersby for a *calaverita*, a small gift of money. They don't knock on people's doors like American kids do on Halloween.

Figures from the Day of the Dead celebration.

dead are brought to Mexico each year by the annual migration of monarch butterflies. The Day of the Dead is a traditional family holiday to honor one's ancestors. While it might seem that this would be a sad day, the Day of the Dead is celebrated as a happy day of remembering. People dress up like ghosts and skeletons, just like we do for Halloween. In fact, the Day of the Dead is at the same time of

Day of the dead motif.

the year as Halloween. Families make altars that they decorate with flowers. Another tradition is for the whole family to go to the cemetery where they clean and then decorate the graves of their ancestors with flowers and candles. At the cemetery there is a picnic with special food.

. . .

Make Your Own MEXICAN ATOLE

1 Stir the masa flour and hot water together.

2 Pour the 5 cups of water and the masa/water mixture into a blender, and blend until smooth. When well blended, pour the mixture into the saucepan and warm on medium heat.

3 Once the mixture has thickened, add the *piloncillo* or brown sugar/molasses and stir until fully dissolved. Remove from the stove and pour into mugs. Sprinkle with cinnamon before serving.

SUPPLIES

½ cup masa flour

¼ cup hot water

5 cups water

blender

medium-sized saucepan

4 tablespoons chopped *piloncillo* (unrefined Mexican brown sugar) OR ¼ cup brown sugar mixed with 2 teaspoons molasses

cinnamon

Make Your Own
REPLICA OF A MAYA CHILD'S TOY

1 Blow up one balloon to form the dog's body. Tie a knot in the neck of the balloon. Blow up a smaller balloon for the dog's head. Attach the smaller balloon to the larger one with masking tape.

2 Use the masking tape to attach the four pieces of cardboard rolls to the larger balloon. These will be the dog's legs. Spread out some newspaper over your work surface.

3 Heat the water in the microwave. Mix the flour into the water until it makes a thick paste. Dip strips of newspaper into the paste, but only as you need them or they will get soggy. Lay the newspaper strips all over the dog form, until you've built up about four layers. This is very messy, but fun!

4 Set your dog aside and let it dry for a couple

of days. You might want to place a cup or other support beneath the head of the dog as it dries so the head will not droop or fall.

5 When your dog is dry, burst the balloons with a sewing needle or a pair of scissors. Paint your dog white or brown (or spotted!). Use black paint to fill in features, such as ears, eyes, tail, and nose. Spray your dog with at least one coat of varnish to make it harder and to keep the paint from chipping.

6 Poke holes through the legs then stick the dowel through them. Attach the wheels to the dowels.

7 Put a little ball of clay at each end of each dowel so the wheels don't come off.

SUPPLIES

2 balloons (and some extras in case of pops!)

masking tape

2 toilet paper rolls cut in half or 1 paper towel roll cut into four pieces (for legs)

6 cups water

3 cups flour

microwave-safe mixing bowl

newspaper cut into thin strips

sewing needle or scissors

¼-inch dowel for wheels (available in hardware or craft stores)

4 wooden wheels (available in craft stores; make sure hole in wheel is large enough for dowel to fit into)

craft paint (black, brown, white)

paint brush

spray varnish

clay

CHAPTER 8

GODS AND SACRIFICES

Every aspect of Maya culture was based on religion. The Maya were polytheists, meaning they worshipped many gods. Maya experts know that the Maya had names for at least 166 gods, and they may have had more. The Maya prayed to these gods every day, and offered their gods blood sacrifices in exchange for favors. While the Maya usually sacrificed animals like dogs, turkeys, squirrels, and iguanas, humans were sacrificed during large community ceremonies, which were held for important requests like good crops.

Perhaps the Maya spilled blood so easily because they believed their gods had done so

The Mayan symbol for *Hunab-Ku*.

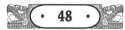

IMPORTANT MAYA GODS

Hunab-Ku: supreme god believed to have created the world.

Itzamná: god of the heavens, who introduced the Maya to writing and medicine.

Chaac: god of agriculture, rain, and lightning.

Kinich-Ahau: god of sun.

Yum-Kaax: god of corn.

Ixchel: goddess of fertility and childbirth.

Yat Balam: god of war.

Ek-Chuah: god of merchants and selling.

Ah-Puch: god of death who ruled over Mitnal, the land of death, the lowest and most horrible of the nine hells.

Chaac

Ah-Puch

first. According to Maya legends, the first humans were created when the gods mixed their blood with maize. For this gift of life, the Maya believed their gods expected blood offerings in return. Without the blood sacrifices, the Maya thought the gods would get angry and destroy the world.

But the Maya also offered blood sacrifices to keep the world from spinning out of control. They believed gods guided the sun and moon across the sky each day. When the earth was cloaked by night, the gods led the sun on a journey through the underworld, threatened by evil gods. The gods leading the moon fought a similar battle during the day. In order to have the strength to win this daily battle, the gods needed human blood. So the Maya made sacrifices each day to their gods. They often made small figurines of their gods, called **fetishes**, which they prayed to.

Because priests and kings had the most access to the gods, they were expected to offer up their own blood.

DID YOU KNOW?

Merchant traders provided kings living far from coastal areas with the shark teeth and stingray spines they used to cut their bodies for blood sacrifices.

WORDS TO KNOW

fetishes: Small figurines that are believed to have magical or spiritual powers.

self-mutilation: Injury or disfigurement to oneself.

fasting: To eat very little or nothing at all. The Maya usually did this for religious purposes.

The ancient Maya believed that their god *Itzamná*, which translates to "Iguana House," gave humans writing, farming, and medicine.

Based on paintings and carvings found by archaeologists, it appears these nobles were experts at **self-mutilation**. Maya kings often used shark teeth and stingray spines to make wounds in their bodies. Stingray spines are angled in one direction—and cause considerable pain if pulled out backward—so they were perfect for the kings to use to pierce their bodies. Royal wives also offered up their blood so they could speak with the gods.

One of the most famous records archaeologists have discovered of kings and queens making blood sacrifices is a carving of Lady Xoc, wife of Yaxchilán king Shield Jaguar, which was made around 725 CE. Shield Jaguar was a powerful warrior who brought many cities under his control. In the carvings, Lady Xoc is shown asking a god to give Shield Jaguar victory in battle. She is pulling cords with thorns through her tongue as Shield Jaguar holds a flaming torch above her. She would have completed this painful act after **fasting** for days, then eating only plants that would have put her into a hallucinogenic state. When she had bled enough to cover strips of bark with her blood, she would have burned the strips. The Maya believed the gods appeared in smoke as it spiraled skyward.

During large community sacrifice ceremonies, when the kings communicated

Lady Xoc, a royal wife, offering up her blood to the gods.

As a result of the ceremonial bloodletting, Lady Xoc has a vision. *Yat Balam*, founder of the Yaxchilán dynasty appears to her in the mouth of a vision serpent.

with the gods in public, community residents played important roles. Men and women danced separately in group dances. They played instruments in complicated musical **processions**. This was serious business. Written records from this period note that the participants were severely punished if they stepped out of beat or hit the wrong note.

The Maya turned to nature for their instruments. For trumpets, they blew into **conch shells**, or carved them from long **gourds** or wood. They also made rattles from the gourds. They hollowed out logs and covered the ends with deerskin to make drums, or made them from large turtle shells and used deer horns for drumsticks. They even made flutes out of clay and the leg bones of deer. But there's one type of instrument the Maya did not make or use. Can you guess what it is? Try to figure out which section of their symphony is missing before you look at the answer that follows.

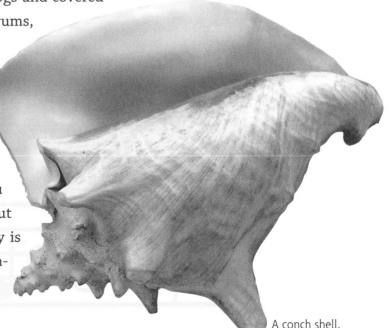

A conch shell.

The Maya did not make stringed instruments.

To purify themselves for the sacrifice ceremonies, the king and priests washed themselves carefully and refused to eat. This practice of not eating for a period of time is called fasting. The priests then painted their bodies blue—the color of water and sky—and they painted their sacrificial victims blue as well. The priests made this paint by blending indigo dye and a type of clay called attapulgite.

During religious ceremonies the priests and kings wore special ceremonial masks and headdresses decorated with the feathers of toucans, parrots, pheasants, and curassows. These feathers represented the gods the priests and kings were trying to contact. The Maya believed that by putting on the headdresses, the priests and kings became the very gods they were trying to look like. The ceremonial headdresses were often taller than the kings and priests. The headdress framework was probably made of wood or papier mâché, and they included a front piece carved to represent one or more of the gods. They were decorated with stones, shells, and the iridescent tail feathers of the quetzal bird.

Kings also wore ceremonial belts made from leather, cloth, and sisal rope that were decorated with shells, beads, and large rectangular pieces of green jadeite. Sometimes the jadeite was carved into the shape of human skulls. Some kings chose to wear real human skulls on their belts! We also know they sometimes wore high sandals woven from cornhusks and sisal fibers.

A Greater Currassow.

WORDS TO KNOW

processions: A group of people moving along in the same direction, to the same place, or for the same reason.

conch shells: Large spiral shells that can be used as horns.

gourds: The dried and hollowed-out shell of plants related to the pumpkin, squash, and cucumber.

When ready to conduct the sacrifices, the priests and kings climbed the steps of their steep pyramids to reach their sacred temples. Unlike the triangle-shaped pyramids in Egypt, Maya pyramids were flat on top. The Maya believed their pyramids represented mountains, and the temples at their flat peaks were caves. It was from this height that the Maya felt closest to their gods living in the sky world.

Although the temple steps were wide across, they were so narrow that it was difficult to walk up them using more than the balls of the feet. Most tourists who climb up and down the pyramids today walk sideways. Many even climb down from the top sitting down, step by step. It is so steep that many people get dizzy. Climbing up and down the steps, in full ceremonial dress, was just one skill the priests and kings had to master!

A clay figure of a king in ceremonial dress.

THE MAYA WORD FOR PYRAMID IS WITZ, WHICH MEANS "MOUNTAIN." THE MAYA BELIEVED MOUNTAINS HOUSED THE SOULS OF THEIR ANCESTORS AND GODS. TO BE CLOSE TO THEM, THE PRIESTS PLACED THE CEREMONIAL ALTARS AT THE TOP OF THEIR PYRAMIDS.

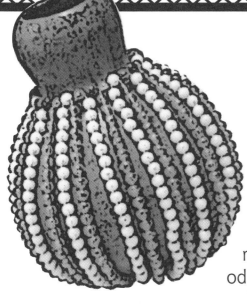

Make Your Own

MUSICAL GOURD

The Maya invented musical instruments based on the natural world. Here are two ways to make a musical gourd. The second method makes a more authentic Maya maraca, but you need time to dry out the gourd.

METHOD 1:

1 Blow up a balloon to form a round or oblong gourd. Tie a knot. Spread newspaper over your work surface.

2 Mix the Celluclay powder with water, following the directions on the packaging. Celluclay acts just like molding clay. Build up the shape of your gourd by applying the clay with your hands. Evenly cover the entire balloon, then set it aside to dry.

3 Use the scissors to cut a hole in one end of the "gourd" to pop the balloon. Enlarge the hole so it is just slightly larger than your stick. Pour about a half cup of dried beans or rice (or both) into the hole.

4 Hold the gourd between your knees so that the hole is facing the ceiling. Carefully slide the stick into the hole so that it goes in about 2 inches. Use a pencil to draw a line around the stick where it meets the gourd. Remove the stick and add a line of hot glue to the pencil line. Carefully slide the stick back in the hole, so that the glue seals the gourd and stick together. This also stops your beans/rice from spilling out. Allow the glue to dry for a few minutes.

stick

SUPPLIES

balloons

newspaper

Celluclay instant papier-mâché paste and water

scissors

stick (long and thick enough to serve as your gourd rattle handle)

dried beans or rice

pencil

hot glue gun

brown, black, yellow paint

paint brush

spray varnish

twine

beads (with holes large enough for the twine to go through)

5 Hold the rattle by the handle and paint the gourd brown. Add more texture to the gourd by adding squiggle lines or speckles with your black and yellow paints. Allow the paint to dry by placing the rattle handle end into a drinking glass.

6 Spray the gourd with at least one coat of varnish to make it shiny. Use your hot glue gun to glue twine strands around the handle. Start at the end of the handle that meets the gourd. Hang beads from the ends of the twine. As you shake the rattle, they'll jump around.

METHOD 2:

1 This project is simple but lots of fun. Hold your gourd by the handle. Have an adult help you use the sharp knife to chop off the top inch or so of the gourd. You'll be gluing the top back on to the gourd, so try to make a clean cut.

2 Use your spoon to scoop out the gourd's insides. Let the gourd dry out for a few days. The drier it is, the better the sound will be.

3 Cut several pieces of twine or string approximately 4 inches long. Tie feathers, shells, or beads to the string. Leave about 1½ inches of the string free.

4 Take the hot glue gun and glue the free end of the string to the inside of the gourd. The end of the string with the feathers and beads will hang over the outside of the gourd.

5 When the strings are glued in place, fill the inside of the gourd with a handful of dry beans, rice, or even gravel. Don't pack the gourd full; allow room for the beans to shake around.

6 Use the hot glue gun to glue the lid of the gourd back on the body of the gourd. When it is dry you'll have a beautiful Maya maraca!

SUPPLIES

gourd—try to find one that has a natural "handle"

sharp knife

spoon

scissors

twine or string

feathers, shells, beads

hot glue gun

dry beans, rice, or gravel

Make Your Own

CLAY GOD FETISHES

HUMAN FACE

1 Cover your work space with wax paper so that the clay will not stick to your table. Roll out the black Sculpey clay to form a thin 2-inch square.

2 Wad the foil up to form a 1-inch rectangle. Roll out either the tan or white Sculpey to make a triangle about 1½ inches across. Cut a long oval piece out of the triangle. This becomes your god's head. Drape the head over the piece of foil so that it is rounded like a real person's face.

3 Lay the head on the flat black piece and push it together gently. Trim the black square so that it is only slightly larger than the head. You can cut the edges straight, or make them wavy or zigzagged.

4 Using the leftovers of your white or tan, make three little logs. These become the mouth and eyes of your god. Also make a small triangle. This becomes the nose of your god. Attach the eye logs to the middle of the head. Then push the nose and mouth into place. Lay a toothpick across the eyes and gently push down. This forms upper and lower eyelids.

5 Add eyeballs by placing two green beads between the eyelids. Make two small holes at the bottom of the nose to create nostrils. Place the brown or black beads around the top of your god's head to create hair.

6 Bake according to the directions on the clay wrapper.

SUPPLIES

wax paper

Sculpey clay—black, tan, white, brown, and green

small rectangle of foil

plastic knife

toothpicks

small green beads

medium black or brown beads

IGUANA

1 Using the brown or green clay, roll a ball of clay into a log about 4 inches long. At one end of the log, push the sides of the clay together to form a triangle shape. This is your iguana's head.

2 Use your toothpick to make two holes for the eyes.

Place two small green beads in the holes.

3 Make a long curved tail from the other end of the log. Make legs by rolling two medium balls of clay into thin logs. If you curve the legs, your iguana will appear to be moving.

4 For more decoration, insert a row of beads down the iguana's backbone. Bake according to the directions on the clay wrapper.

CHAPTER 9

POK·A·TOK

One of the most well-known games the Maya played was a fast and furious ball game called *Pok-A-Tok*. *Pok-A-Tok* is believed to have been invented around 2000 BCE, and was played in every major Maya city. Teams were usually made up of one to four players, who often worked in pairs. The object of the game was to get a ball through a narrow stone hoop that was located on the court wall, sometimes as high up as 20 feet from the ground. Players could not use their hands or feet—only their head, shoulders, elbows, wrists, and hips.

An intense game of *Pok-A-Tok*.

Pok-A-Tok was a challenging game, but for the Maya, it was more than a game: it symbolized the struggle of life over death, and war and hunting. Often, *Pok-A-Tok* was played by prisoners who had been captured in battle, and the losing team was sacrificed to the gods. Games would go on for very long periods of time, sometimes for days. It was so difficult to score that if a player actually got the ball through the ring on the wall, the game usually ended.

The Maya sometimes played the game just for fun. Players wore a lot of protective padding around their waists, and on one shin and forearm. They did so because the game's hard, solid-rubber ball could seriously hurt or kill them. The balls were made from rubber from *cau-uchu* trees, and drawings and paintings of the game show that the ball was about as big as a basketball is today. The padding, called yokes, was made of cotton stuffed into wooden frames. We know this because one of these yokes was found in a tomb at Tikal. Yet

The great ball court at Chichén Itzá.

THE AMAZING RUBBER TREE

Archaeologists have learned that many Mesoamerican people used rubber by 1600 BCE. Rubber was grown in the rainforest of the lowlands, and then traded to surrounding areas. It wasn't just used for making balls. Rubber was used to attach stones to wooden handles, to seal bags that carried water, to waterproof clothing, and to make drumsticks for wooden drums. The Maya even coated their feet with layers of rubber to make a type of shoe. Rubber was also used by the shaman-priests to treat lip and ear wounds. To harvest rubber, the Maya made diagonal cuts in the bark of *cau-uchu* trees to start the flow of latex down a central vertical channel and into their containers. Experts believe the rubber was combined with the juice of the morning glory vine to make it solidify into a solid mass. This made the rubber tough, strong, and very elastic—perfect for bouncing. Before it hardened, which it did within minutes, the Maya were able to shape the rubber into whatever size ball they wanted. We know some of their rubber balls were as large as a basketball.

even in games of fun, the losing team (or at least the captain), was usually sacrificed. Would you want to play *Pok-A-Tok* given those odds?

The largest ball court in Mesoamerica is at the ruins of Chichén Itzá, in Mexico's Yucatán peninsula. The Great Ballcourt of Chichén Itzá is 545 feet long and 225 feet wide. The court walls are lined with carvings depicting the sacrifices made at the game's end. Next to the court is a stone platform decorated with hundreds of carved skulls—a visual reminder that many players lost their heads.

One of three ball-court markers at Copán from the center of the playing field shown in the diagram at the left.

Make Your Own

RUBBER BALL

This activity will show you two ways to make a rubber ball of your own. The first method is easier and faster, but the second method is more authentic because it is all rubber.

METHOD 1:

1 Take a sheet of aluminum foil and crumple it into a ball. The foil ball can be any size, but the larger it is, the more rubber bands you'll need to cover it. You can also use just rubber bands by starting off with several rubber bands doubled up and wrapped around each other.

2 Stretch rubber bands over the foil one at a time until it's completely covered. Make sure you stretch the rubber bands completely around the ball so it stays as round as possible. Add each rubber band at a different angle so that your ball grows in an even way.

SUPPLIES

Method 1:

aluminum foil

rubber bands

METHOD 2:

This project should be done in a ventilated area!

1 Spread a thin layer of rubber cement on a flat surface. Let it dry for a few minutes.

2 Start pushing your fingers around on the tacky rubber cement. It will peel off and gradually stick together. Roll it around into a ball.

3 Spread another layer of rubber cement on your work surface. After it's dried for a few minutes, roll your ball around on the new layer. It will peel up and stick to your ball. Keep rolling it around and all the rubber cement will gradually form into a bigger ball.

4 Repeat this process as many times as you like, building up your rubber ball.

SUPPLIES

jar of rubber cement

brush

Play a Version of
POK·A·TOK

The rules of this version of *Pok-A-Tok* are very simple, and you can play by yourself or with friends.

1 Draw a circle about 5 inches in diameter onto each piece of paper. If you are playing by yourself you will only need one piece of paper.

2 Tape or tack a piece of paper on opposite walls slightly above your head to start. While you can start the game at any height, remember that the higher the target, the more challenging the game will be.

SUPPLIES

two pieces of paper

pencil or pen

tape

a ball

3 Divide into two equal teams and choose your targets. Working as a team, try to hit the center of the circle on your team's target with the rubber ball WITHOUT using your hands. The other team will try to take the ball away from you to hit their target, but they also cannot use their hands.

4 The first team to hit the target wins a point. When both teams have scored a point on their target, move the target higher. Or make the game more challenging by only using your feet, legs, and head. Imagine trying to play *Pok-A-Tok* like the Maya did, with a heavy rubber ball and a 30-foot-high ring—and remember the penalty for losing in ancient Maya culture was death!

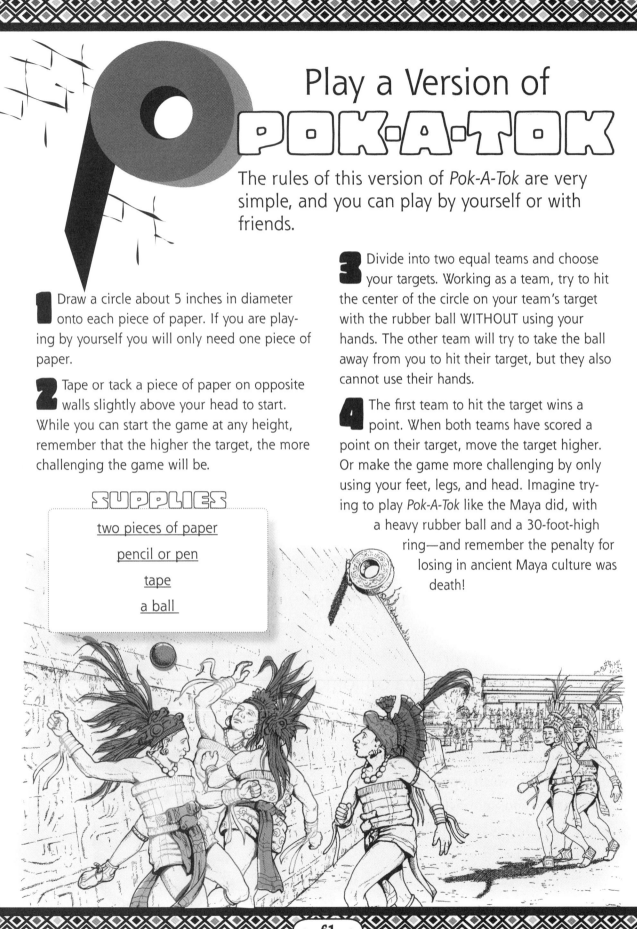

CHAPTER 10

NUMBERS

All Maya people learned to count. Both their calendars and counting system were based on the number 20. Farmers used the counting system when planting and harvesting crops, merchants used it when buying and selling goods, and builders used it to take measurements and determine angles. Their precise measurements made for sturdy structures, which is evident today in the ruins of Maya buildings.

Maya numbers were made up of just three symbols: a shell, which indicated zero; a dot, which represented the number one; and a bar, which represented the number five. It was very easy to add, subtract, and multiply whole numbers using this number system. The Maya didn't worry about fractions like we do.

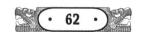

Here's how the Maya wrote numbers 0 through 19:

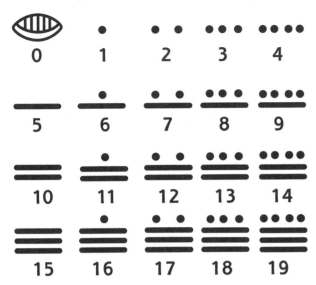

If the Maya wanted to add or multiply larger numbers, they used "steps" that represented a multiplication of 20. That means the number written on step two was 20 times more than the number on step one. And the number written on step three was 20 times more than the number on step two.

Numbers 1 through 19 were on the lowest step, numbers 20 through 399 were placed on the second step, numbers 400 through 7,999 were placed on the third step, and numbers 8,000 through 159,999 were placed on the fourth step. The Maya just kept adding steps to get to the number they wanted—even up to the hundreds of millions!

Make Your Own
MAYA COUNTING FLASH CARDS

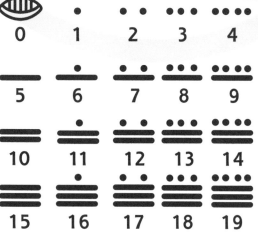

0	1	2	3	4
5	6	7	8	9
10	11	12	13	14
15	16	17	18	19

1 Copy the Maya number symbols in the chart above onto 20 index cards. On the back of each card, write the number for that symbol.

2 "Laminate" the cards with a layer of the clear packing tape on the front and back. This will keep the cards from getting dirty and crumpled.

3 Hold each card up to two friends and see who guesses the number first. You already know the answer because you've written it on the back of the card!

4 Once this game becomes too easy, try playing with two cards at the same time. Up the ante by making your friends add, subtract, or multiply the two numbers.

5 If you make two decks, you can even play the game "Concentra-tion." Cover up the number on the back of the card with a small post-it sticker that's easy to remove. Place the 40 cards face down on the floor. When you correctly match two of the same card, you win the pair. Go again! The player with the most pairs at the end of the game wins. You can even use the cards to play a game of "Go Fish" or "War."

SUPPLIES

index cards

pencil or pen

tape

a ball

IF THE MAYA WANTED TO COUNT LARGER NUMBERS, THEY JUST KEEP ADDING STEPS THAT MULTIPLIED THE NUMBER 20 BY ITSELF. THE MAYA USED NAMES TO SIGNIFY THE INCREASED VALUES OF 20: *KAL* (20), *BAK* ($20^2 = 400$), *PIC* ($20^3 = 8,000$), *CALAB* ($20^4 = 160,000$), *KINCHIL* ($20^5 = 3,200,000$), AND *ALAU* ($20^6 = 64,000,000$).

Here's how the Maya would have written the number 14:

$$\overset{\bullet\;\bullet\;\bullet\;\bullet}{\equiv} \;+\; — \;=\; \overset{\bullet\;\bullet\;\bullet\;\bullet}{\equiv}$$

(9 + 5 = 14)

When they were adding numbers on different steps, the Maya wrote them atop each other. So, to write the number 32, the Maya put two bars and a dot on the first step (12) and a dot on the second step (20 x 1). Here's how it would look:

20s   •
       (20)

1s $\overset{\bullet\;\;\bullet}{=}$ 
     (12)

When the Maya wrote the number 407, they used the third step. Here they used the zero as a place holder when there was no number needed on a step. They wrote a bar and two dots on the first step (7), a zero on the second step (0 x 20), and a dot on the third step (1 x 400). It looks like this:

400s •
      (400)

20s 👁 
     (0)

1s $\overset{\bullet\;\;\bullet}{—}$
    (7)

If the Maya wanted to write the number 8,003, they put three dots on the first step (3), a zero on the second step (0 x 20), a zero on the third step (0 x 400), and a dot on the fourth step (1 x 8,000).

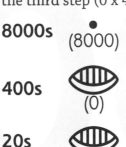

8000s (8000)

400s (0)

20s (0)

1s (3)

Figure Out Your Own MAYA NUMBERS

Have you got the hang of it yet?! See if you can figure out the totals for these number glyphs:

A.

B.

C.

D.

A._____   B._____

C._____   D._____

Let's make the game harder. How would you write these numbers in glyph form?

E. 1,000   **F.** 58   **G.** 381   **H.** 56,000

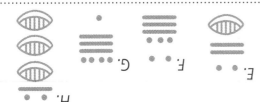

H.

G.

F.

E.

CHAPTER II

CALENDARS

When archaeologists and other experts first began to study ancient Maya hieroglyphs, they were very confused. At first they thought the figures were gods. But then a German librarian named Ernst Forstemann figured out that some of the symbols stood for numbers. With this knowledge, experts began to figure out the Maya calendar. They quickly realized that the ancient Maya were obsessed with time. Maya calendars were the most complex in Mesoamerica and were more accurate than calendars being used in Europe at that time.

Maya priests kept track of time by watching the skies. Lacking the telescopes we have today, they used

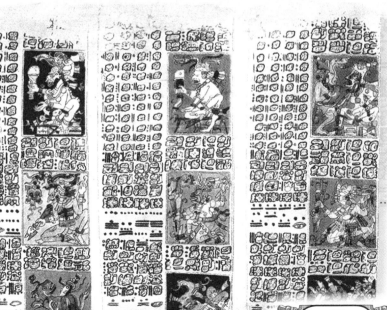

Pages from the Dresden Codex.

Carving on an altar in Copán that is believed to be Maya astronomers attending a convention around 776 CE to correct the calendar.

only a forked stick and their naked eye to track the movements of stars and planets. They were even able to calculate when the planets would align and when solar eclipses would occur. We know this because they recorded this astrological information in special books called **codices**.

The Maya believed their gods moved the planets. They considered Venus to be the most important planet. They called it "*Nok Ek*," which means "Great Star," because it was so bright that it was visible to the naked eye. They also thought the planet was linked to their serpent god *Kukulcán*, and Maya kings went to war based on its position. To the Maya, war was not just a clash of people and weapons but a battle of spirits. Priests also made predictions about the future when Venus appeared. They believed the night skies told them the best days for couples to marry and have children, what children should be named, and when human sacrifices should take place.

The head of the serpent god *Kukulcán*.

The ancient Maya relied primarily on two calendars for everyday life: the *tzolk'in* calendar, also called the Sacred Round, and the **haab**, also called the Vague Year. Experts believe these calendars date back to the sixth century BCE. Both calendars were based on 20-day months. The Maya priests used the two calendars together to create a calendar of 52 years called the Calendar Round.

Mayan glyph for *Imix.*

The *tzolk'in* was used to decide spiritual matters, such as when ceremonies should be held. The priests assigned each calendar day, called **k'in**, a god name and a number between 1 and 13. The day names, with their English translations, are *Imix* (waterlily), *Ik* (wind), *Ak'bal* (night), *K'an* (corn), *Chicchan* (snake), *Cimi* (death head), *Manik* (hand), *Lamat* (Venus), *Muluc* (water), *Oc* (dog), *Chuen* (frog), *Eb* (skull), *Ben* (corn stalk), *Ix* (jaguar), *Men* (eagle), *Cib* (shell), *Caban* (earth), *Etz'nab* (flint), *Cauac* (storm cloud), and *Ahau* (lord).

Mayan glyph for *Ik.*

The Maya would have written the hieroglyphs for the god names like this:

1 *Imix* 2 *Ik* 3 *Ak'bal* 4 *K'an* 5 *Chicchan* 6 *Cimi* 7 *Manik*

8 *Lamat* 9 *Muluc* 10 *Oc* 11 *Chuen* 12 *Eb* 13 *Ben* 1 *Ix*

2 *Men* 3 *Cib* 4 *Caban* 5 *Etz'nab* 6 *Cauac* 7 *Ahau*

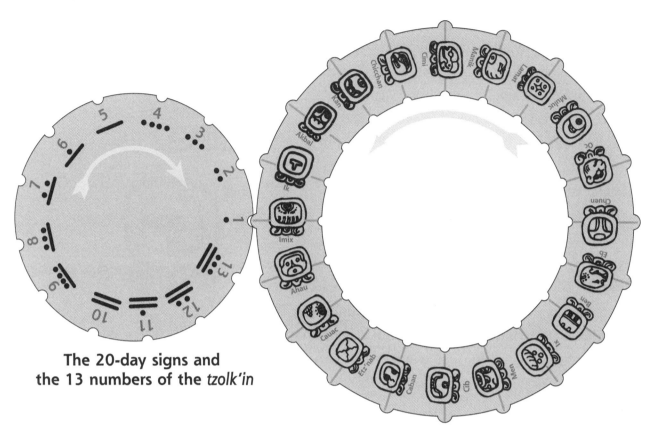

**The 20-day signs and
the 13 numbers of the *tzolk'in***

As you can see, the first day of the calendar began with the first number and first name: 1 *Imix*. The second day was 2 *Ik*. The 13th day was 13 *Ben*. But then the numbers ran out and started over. So, day 14 was 1 *Ix*. As the numbers cycled through the 20 names, it took the full 260-days for the *tzolk'in* calendar to start over at 1 *Imix*.

The haab calendar was based on a 365-day solar cycle. This is the number of days in the calendar we use. The priests used the haab to decide when farmers should plant their crops. The calendar wasn't perfectly exact, as it didn't account for a leap year. The haab had 18 months that were each 20 days long. The names of the 18 months were *Pop, Uo, Zip, Zotz, Zec, Xul, Yaxkin, Mol, Ch'en, Yax, Zac, Ceh, Mac, Kankin, Muan, Pax, Kayab*, and *Cumku*:

But 18 months multiplied by 20 days

DID YOU KNOW?

The Maya believed that a person's birth date decided if they would have good luck or bad luck in life. Maya born on the days of well-wishing gods were considered lucky. But those born on days with evil gods had to offer many sacrifices to earn their luck!

is only 360 days. Where are the other 5 days? The Maya added these unlucky days, called *uayeb,* to the end of the calendar. On these unlucky days, the Maya didn't eat and they offered many sacrifices. They also didn't do any work, to make sure the gods didn't harm them.

Use the haab glyph symbols included here to see how this calendar worked. The haab started with the number 0, so the first day would have been 0 *Pop*. The second day would have been 1 *Pop*. Day 20 would have been 19 *Pop*. With that, all of the 20 days in the *Pop* month would have been used up, so the next day would start with the month *Uo*. Each day of the 18 months had their turn, as well as the five unlucky days, before the calendar started over.

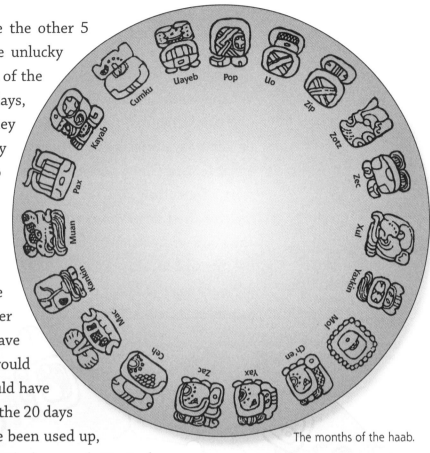

The months of the haab.

When the priests used the *tzolk'in* and the haab calendars together as the Calendar Round, they could see 18,980 days (52 years) at one time. In the Calendar Round, the two calendars rotated together, like cogged wheels, and the dates from each calendar were combined. The first day of the Calendar Round was 1 *Imix* 0 *Pop*. As the Calendar Round had to cycle through all 18,980 days, it took the full 52 years for 1 *Imix* 0 *Pop* to line up again. The Maya referred to these 52-year periods as "bundles," much like we call 100-year periods "centuries."

DID YOU KNOW?

The Long Count was primarily based on the number 20.

1 *k'in* = 1 day
20 *k'ins* = 1 *winal* (month)
18 *winals* = 1 *tun* (360 days)
20 *tuns* = 1 *k'atun* (7,200 days)
20 *ka'tuns* = 1 *bak'tun* (144,000 days or 400 years)

At the end of the 52-year cycle, there was what the Maya believed to be a sacred day. The Maya feared this day, as they believed the sky would fall on them if the gods were unhappy with humans.

A third calendar, called the **Long Count**, was used only by Maya priests and scribes. They used this calendar to record long periods of time—even from the start of creation. Thirteen *bak'tun*, one complete cycle of the Long Count, equaled 1,872,000 days! The Maya wrote dates in this order: *bak'tun, k'atun, tun, winal, k'in*. This calendar was so hard to figure out that the Maya commoners left it to the priests and scribes.

WORDS TO KNOW

codices: Handwritten books in which the Maya recorded their history. Only three originals remain.

tzolk'in or Sacred Round: A period of 260 days constituting a complete cycle of all the permutations of 20 day names with the numbers 1 to 13 that constitutes the Maya sacred year.

haab or Vague Year: The 365-day year of the Maya calendar.

Long Count: A complex calendar only used by Maya priests and scribes (because it was so challenging to understand) to record very long periods of time—even from the start of creation.

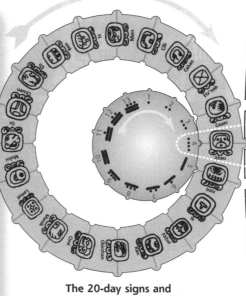

The 20-day signs and the 13 numbers of the *tzolk'in*

Date to be read as 4 *Ahau* 8 *Cumku*

The haab, the 365-day Vague Year

Seating of Cumku, the last day of *Kayab*

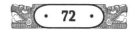

Make Your Own
TZOLK'IN CALENDAR WHEEL

1 Use your mathematical compass to draw two circles on your piece of cardstock: one with a diameter of 6 inches and the other with a diameter of 4 inches. Cut out both circles.

2 Cut out the 20 *tzolk'in* glyphs. Glue them along the outer edge of the large circle, in the right order, making sure they're evenly spaced and facing in the same direction.

3 Write the glyphs for the numbers 1 through 13 evenly spaced along the edge of the small circle.

4 Lay the two circles next to each other on your table. Line the number 1 up with the first month, *Imix*. Roll the number circle around the day circle, so that you see that day two is 2 *Ik*, day three is 3 *Ak'bal* . . . and day 13 is 13 *Ben*. What is the date of the 14th day? Yes! It's 1 *Ix*, because the numbers start over. But what's the 27th day? And the 40th? And the 53rd?

Figure Out Your Own

SUPPLIES

paper

pencil

colored markers

Using the *tzolk'in* and haab glyphs included in this section, draw the glyphs for these Calendar Round dates:

8 *Ben* 14 *Pax* (day 8 *Ben* of the *tzolk'in* and 6th *Pax* month of the haab)

2 *Cauac* 4 *Zip* (day 2 *Cauac* of the *tzolk'in* and 4th *Zip* month of the haab)

1 *Ik* 19 *Pop* (day 1 *Ik* of the *tzolk'in* and 8th *Pop* month of the haab)

SUPPLIES

heavy construction paper or poster board

pencil

Elmer's glue

fine-tip paintbrush

different colors of colored sand (available in craft stores)

plastic container and spoon for each sand color

hair spray or artist's fixative

Make Your Own SAND ART PICTURE OF THE COSMOS

1 Use a pencil to draw a picture of the stars and planets on the construction paper or poster board. Remember that really small shapes are hard to fill in with sand. Decide where you want to put each sand color, and write the first letter of the color so you'll remember where it should go.

2 With your paintbrush, apply an even layer of glue to a small section of your design. It's important to work on small sections so the glue doesn't dry out before you can cover it with sand.

3 Use the plastic spoon to pour a small amount of the colored sand onto the glue. You can spread it out with your finger, if necessary. Hold your paper over the sand container and tap it so the excess sand slides back into the container. You can also put all the excess sand in one container to make multicolored sand.

4 Repeat these steps until your entire design is finished. Let it dry. To "set" your sand painting, lightly spray it with hair spray or artist's fixative.

CHAPTER 12

MAJESTIC BUILDERS

By their classic period (250–900 CE), the ancient Maya had built impressive cities and miles of roadways. In fact, the ancient Maya were the best road builders in Mesoamerica. Some of their roads have survived to this day. Maya engineers and laborers even considered how the rainy season would affect the roads. Why? They didn't want them to get washed away. In swampy areas, roads were built high above the ground to protect them from flooding.

The ancient Maya were careful to build their roads level. They may have used a **plumb bob**, a simple tool they used in building their pyramids. The plumb bob is one of the oldest building tools in the world. It is easily made by hanging a heavy weight from a cord. When the plumb bob hung straight, the Maya knew their horizontal and vertical lines were straight.

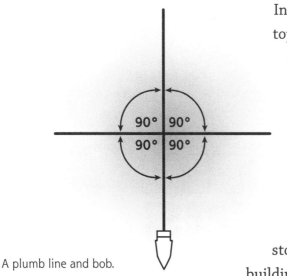

A plumb line and bob.

In the city squares, Maya laborers built tall pyramids topped with temples and sacrificial altars. Workers also built *Pok-A-Tok* ball courts, bathhouses, and buildings used to conduct official city business. Tall observatories were constructed where priests could study the night skies and make their predictions. And laborers built stone palaces and homes for members of the large royal families.

The ancient Maya used limestone for most of their important city buildings, as it was strong and there was plenty of it available. Workers **quarried** large blocks of limestone from the ground using chisels with sharp flint and obsidian blades. These stone blades were attached to wooden handles, and easily cut through the limestone. How could these tools cut through stone so easily? Limestone has an interesting quality—it is soft when buried underground but it hardens when it is dug up and exposed to the air.

After cutting the limestone from the **bedrock**, Maya laborers pried the blocks loose using wooden mallets and wedges. They then had to transport the blocks from the quarries back to their cities. They didn't have wheeled carts or horses, so they pulled the blocks across the ground with rope, or rolled them along the tops of

An obsidian blade.

WORDS TO KNOW

plumb bob: A weight on the end of a line, used especially by masons and carpenters to establish exact vertical and horizontal lines.

quarry: To dig or cut rock from the earth.

bedrock: The solid rock earth, well beneath the softer surface of soil, sand, clay, gravel, or water.

mortar: A building material that hardens when it dries, used to hold bricks and stones together like glue.

stucco: A durable finish for exterior walls, usually made of a mixture of cement, sand, limestone, and water, that is applied while wet.

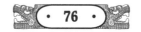

MAYA WHEELS

Did the Maya know about the wheel? Experts think they did. The ancient Maya probably didn't use wheeled carts because the land was so rough and uneven. The carts would have had to be pushed up hills, and probably would have gotten stuck in muddy and marshy areas. The Maya didn't have pack animals, such as donkeys and horses, so they would have had to pull the carts themselves. The only animal the Maya could have used to carry goods was the llama, but llamas are not sturdy enough to pull wheeled carts. Yet the Maya did put wheels on their children's toys! Some experts believe the wheels were clay disks from spindle whorls, which the Maya used to weave raw cotton into thread.

A child's clay jaguar pull-toy with wheels.

logs. Sometimes they floated the blocks down the rivers on rafts.

Buildings were constructed from limestone blocks, held together with thick, quick-drying **mortar** made from limestone or seashells. The mortar was made by putting pieces of limestone or quantities of shells into large bonfires. The heat of the fire reduced the stone or shells to a fine powder. This powder was mixed with gravel and water to make the mortar.

When this mortar was thinned out with a bit more water it became **stucco**, which was the plaster-like material applied to walls, stairways, and doorways. Because stucco was softer than mortar, the workers who specialized in carving could easily carve religious designs and glyph symbols into it. Maya carvers didn't waste time or effort when they went about their work: if only one side of a building was viewed during religious ceremonies, then only that side was decorated. When the carvings were finished, laborers painted the walls a bright red, which made them stand out from the

WORKERS WHO SPECIALIZED IN CARVING WERE CALLED *AH UXUL.* THEY OFTEN WORKED IN GROUPS ON BUILDING PROJECTS OR WHEN CARVING SYMBOLS INTO THE STONE SLABS CALLED STELAE. EXPERTS KNOW THIS BECAUSE SOME STELAE HAVE GROUP SIGNATURES.

green of the trees and the blue of the sky. The paint wore off many, many years ago, which is why Maya ruins look gray today.

Stucco was also used to protect buildings from the humidity of the rainforests. A thick layer of stucco helped to seal the buildings against the rains that fell during the seven rainy months. Builders in these cities used stone rubble to build the foundations of their buildings, as limestone would not have held up against year after year of heavy rains and flooding.

Carvers also used stucco to add decorative touches to the roof combs they built atop pyramids and other important buildings. Roof combs are blocks of stone added to building roofs to make the structures appear taller than they actually are. In some Maya cities, such as Tikal, roof combs are often taller than the buildings they sit on! Because they were so high, roof combs were also quite heavy. To support their great weight, the Maya built roof combs over the thickest walls of the buildings. Many roof combs were also made with vaulted stone corbel arches, rather than solid stone, to reduce their weight and give them an open look.

The corbel arch was used a lot by Maya

A roof comb atop a temple.

builders. In addition to being used for roof combs, it was used in buildings to create doorways, corridors, and peaked rooms. Maya arches were more triangular in shape, not curved like European arches of the time. The corbel arch is a perfect example of the technical skill of the ancient Maya. Not only did the engineers and builders have to understand the stress the stone blocks put on each other, they had to figure out how wide, high, and thick to make each block. They even had to factor in the amount of space the limestone mortar took up between each stone block.

A drawing by Frederick Catherwood of the gateway at Labna (also known as Labna Vault) with its corbel arch.

Corbel arches are tricky to build as there's a lot of pressure put on the arch stones by the rest of the wall. To make sure the arches didn't topple, the Maya built them with thick walls.

Ancient Maya engineers designed buildings to be impressive on the outside. They cared much less about how

Close-up drawing of how stones in corbel arches are fitted together.

DID YOU KNOW?

King Pacal's tomb remained sealed for 1,269 years, until 1948 when a Mexican archaeologist by the name of Alberto Ruz Lhuillier discovered the secret stairway. It took his team 4 years to remove all the rubble the ancient Maya laborers had carted in to protect Pacal II's heavily jeweled corpse. They finally opened the doorway to the tomb in 1952!

THE PURPOSE OF PYRAMIDS

Maya pyramids were built for religious purposes, with temples on their flat tops. They had staircases up the sides that were very, very steep. Priests would climb to the top of the pyramids, to the temples, to perform sacrifices and other rituals. The Maya believed that temples on top of pyramids were closer to the gods. They were also so high that they could be seen from far away.

Some of the pyramids contained the burial tombs of important Maya kings. One king with a tomb in a pyramid was Pacal II, also known as Pacal the Great, who ruled the great city of Palenque. Standing about 100 feet tall, Pacal's burial pyramid is called the Temple of Inscriptions.

When Pacal II died in 683 CE, his body was carried up the pyramid's outer steps and down an 80-foot interior stairway that led to his crypt. Five victims were sacrificed outside the door of his tomb. Workers then sealed off the tomb by filling the stairway with stone rubble. They carried the heavy stones in baskets on their backs that were attached to *tumplines*.

The lid of Pacal's sarcophagus depicting the king and the tree of life.

The Temple of Inscriptions.

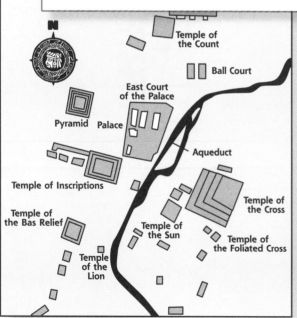

comfortable and impressive-looking the buildings were on the inside. Some experts believe the Maya built for one reason only: to create lavish stages for their city-wide ceremonies when human sacrifices were made to the gods. The eyes of thousands of city residents would have been glued to the kings and priests as they climbed the steep pyramid steps to the sacred sacrificial altars. Imagine how impressive this sight must have been amid the din of blaring horns, pounding drums, and people shouting!

WATCH THE SPIRIT SNAKE SLITHER!

The most famous example of a Maya building with sacred "power" is a pyramid at the ruins of Chichén Itzá, a large city-state that thrived in the northern lowlands between 700 and 900 CE. At the top of this pyramid is a temple called El Castillo, the Spanish term for "the Castle."

The temple of El Castillo was dedicated to *Kukulkán*, the Feathered Serpent god. *Kukulkán* is known as *Quetzalcoatl* to the Olmec and Aztec. Each staircase faces a direction on a compass. There are staircases leading up the four sides of the pyramid. If you add up the 91 steps of each staircase, you get the number 364, but if you also add in the flat platform at the top of the pyramid, you get 365—the number of days in the haab, the Maya solar calendar. Each side of the pyramid has 52 rectangular panels, which is equal to one "bundle" or cycle of 52 years.

At the vernal and autumnal equinoxes each year (around March 21 and September 22) thousands of tourists gather on the northwest side of El Castillo. During the equinox, day and night are about the same length all around the world. On these days, as the sun gradually illuminates the stairs of El Castillo, spectators are treated to a solar phenomenon: it appears that a shadow snake is slithering down the steps from the heavens to earth!

The ancient Maya did not build their cities according to a master plan. But they did align their ceremonial buildings with the points of the compass. They did this to make sure the gods saw their cities as sacred places. As cities grew larger, new buildings were added in proper alignment to the stars. As archaeologists have discovered, new buildings were often built over old buildings.

While workers built massive temples for their kings, they built simple homes of mud and thatch for themselves,

and covered them with stucco so that their houses would hold up better during the rainy season. It is unclear why the commoners didn't get to live in stone houses, but it probably had to do with cost and the fact that wealthy and important members of Maya society kept the limestone for themselves.

Mud homes were certainly easier to build than stone houses. To build a mud home, the Maya packed down a raised platform of dirt with their feet. A retaining

A typical present-day Maya hut.

TREES VITAL TO THE MAYA

Though the ancient Maya built their important city structures out of stone, as a society they were very dependent on trees. Wood from trees fueled fires, which were necessary to cook food, keep warm, and make limestone powder. Without trees, the Maya would have been unable to make their canoes, the handles for tools, many of their musical instruments, and paper for the codices! Without trees, many of the birds and animals who relied on their seeds and foliage for food and shelter would have died. Without cacao trees, Maya kings would not have had access to cacao beans or their favorite chocolate drink. And without trees to hold the soil in place, much of land would have washed away with the rains during the long rainy season.

wall of stones held the raised platform in place. The laborers then used wooden poles to make the walls and the peaked roofs of their houses. They added layers of mud and then stucco over the poles. To shield the interiors from rain, they layered palm thatch or grass onto their peaked roofs. The high peak in the roof's center helped to funnel rainwater off the roof and away from the house.

Were the nobles' homes better to live in? Absolutely. The stone kept their houses warm when it was cold outside and cool during the midday heat. And, as stone doesn't burn, the nobles didn't have to worry about kitchen fires as much as the common workers did. And then there's the pest issue: insects really like wood and grass! Because commoners had more bugs in their homes, they probably got sick a lot more often than nobles did.

ONE PARTICULARLY NASTY BUG IN CENTRAL AMERICA IS THE ASSASSIN BUG. IT CAN CAUSE A DEADLY DISEASE CALLED CHAGAS' DISEASE, BY TRANSMITTING A PARASITE.

Make Your Own

RUIN MAP OF THE MAYA HOMELAND

1 On your piece of cardboard, draw the outline of the ancient Maya homeland using the image on the next page as a guide. Be sure to leave room for the Pacific Ocean, the Caribbean Sea, and the Gulf of Mexico. Set this map aside.

2 Cut little diamonds out of your paper to make flags to identify the Maya ruins of Chichén Itzá, Tikal, Palenque, Tulum, and Copán. Wrap the edge of the flags around the toothpicks with a bit of Elmer's glue.

3 In a mixing bowl, combine the flour, salt, and lemon juice. Slowly add water to create your salt dough. If the dough is too dry, add more water. If it is too sticky, add a bit more flour.

4 Use your spoon to spread the dough across your map. Carefully fill in all of the land area, but leave the water areas uncovered. It is okay that the map surface is bumpy, as it represents land!

SUPPLIES

large piece of thick cardboard—the lid of a pizza box would be perfect

pencil

paper

scissors

toothpicks

Elmer's glue

mixing bowl

2 cups all-purpose flour

1 cup table salt

1 tablespoon lemon juice

1 cup water

plastic spoon

craft paints (blue plus at least three other colors)

fine-tip black marker (for writing the names of the countries on strips of paper)

paint brush

decorations: beads, feathers, glitter, etc.

MEXICO	GUATEMALA
BELIZE	HONDURAS

EL SALVADOR

5 Use a toothpick to draw the borders that separate modern-day Mexico, Guatemala, Belize, Honduras, and El Salvador. You can decorate the borders with beads or glitter.

6 On little rectangles of paper, write the name of each country. Use your finger to press the strip of paper into the dough on the appropriate areas of your map. Use your imagination to make the names stand out and look interesting.

7 Stick the toothpicks with the ruin names into the map. You can cut the toothpicks in half, if you want the flags to be shorter.

8 Set your map aside for several days, until the dough has dried and hardened. The thicker your "land," the longer it will take to dry.

9 Once the dough is hard, paint the countries different colors. Use blue to color in the Pacific Ocean, Caribbean Sea, and Gulf of Mexico. Label these bodies of water with your marker. Let the paint dry.

10 To seal the dough, so that your map will last longer, mix 1 tablespoon of Elmer's glue with 1 tablespoon of water. Use a paint brush to paint this mixture all over the salt dough to keep it from absorbing moisture.

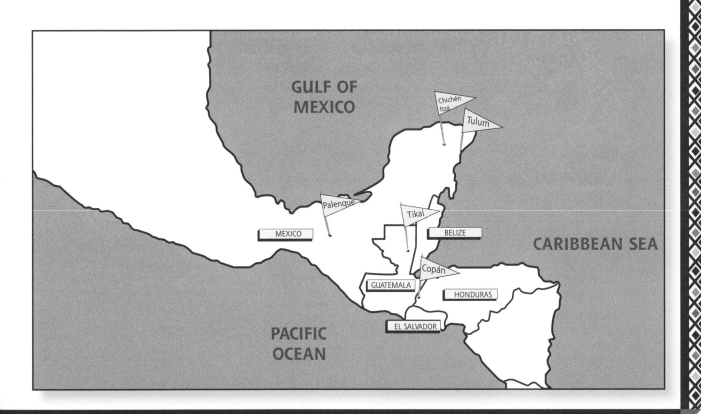

Make Your Own MODEL OF A MAYA PYRAMID

1 Use your ruler and pencil to draw an equilateral (all sides equal) triangle on your piece of paper. Make each side at least 6 inches long.

2 Cut out your triangle pattern and trace its shape onto each of four pieces of cardboard. Cut out each cardboard triangle, then stack them on top of each other. These will be the sides of your pyramid.

3 Draw a line across the top of each triangle, and cut off the top of each triangle at that height. Remember, the Maya built temples with flat tops! Set aside the snipped-off pieces—you'll need these to make the temple at the top of the pyramid.

4 Tape the four triangles together as shown. Turn over the taped triangles, fold them at the hinges, and stand it up. The tape should be on the inside.

5 From a scrap of one of the pieces of cardboard, cut a square big enough to cover the hole at the top of your pyramid. This will be the base of your temple.

6 In one of the four small triangles you set aside to make your temple, cut a small rectangle for a door. Tape these triangles together the same way you taped together the larger pieces.

7 Use your paintbrush to spread glue on the bottom of your temple walls. Place it atop the pyramid and allow the glue to set for a few minutes.

8 Cut four strips of paper about 1 inch wide and 8 inches long. Fold each like an accordion for steps. Attach each with glue to the center of a pyramid side. Allow the glue to set.

9 Cover your work surface with the newspaper, and then spread a thin coat of glue on one side of the pyramid and steps. Sprinkle red sand on top of the glue. Do this with the other three sides and the top. This will give the pyramid its distinctive red Maya appearance.

base of temple

SUPPLIES

ruler

pencil

piece of paper

scissors

5 sheets of thin cardboard (the backs of old pads of paper are perfect!)

masking tape

glue

paintbrush

newspaper

red sand

CHAPTER 13

HIEROGLYPHS

One of the most impressive accomplishments of the Maya was their complex writing system. In fact, of the many societies that lived in Mesoamerica, from the early Olmec to the Aztec, only the Maya developed a complete system of written communication. This means that only the Maya could write down every syllable of their spoken language. The task of writing was given to Maya scribes, who wrote in hieroglyphs. The hieroglyphs look like very detailed drawings of human and animal faces, circles, squares, and squiggly lines.

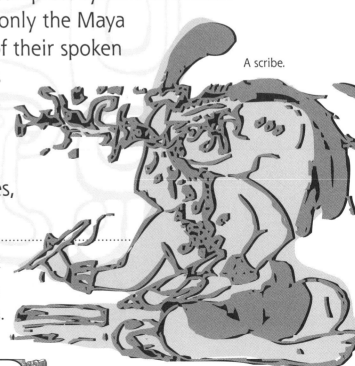

A scribe.

Scribes helped priests record their calculations and predictions from studying the movements of the planets, moon, and stars.

DID YOU KNOW?

The ancient Mayan written language is a complex system of sounds, pictures, and logograms. A logogram is a written character that represents a meaning or word. Some of the hieroglyphs represent individual syllables, some are pictures that represent a word or idea, and some represent a spoken word or phrase.

Another important job of the scribes was to keep records of important events, such as wars and the birth of sons to the king. The scribes wrote in hieroglyphs, which were picture symbols that stood for words. As Mayan writing took considerable skill and memory, scribes enjoyed a prominent position at court. Both men and women were scribes, and many of them were members of the royal family. This allowed them to attend schools that taught them to write. Scribes wore their own distinctive costume and headdress, which announced to every-one who saw them that they possessed their special skill. In the many remaining Maya wall murals and pottery, scribes are shown with stick bundles in their headdresses. The stick bundles represented the tools of their trade: brush pens and quills.

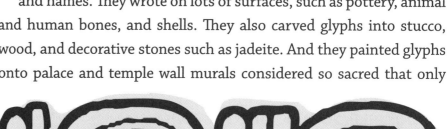

The Mayan glyph for *book*.

Scribes used hieroglyphs to communicate numbers, dates, objects, titles, events, places, and names. They wrote on lots of surfaces, such as pottery, animal and human bones, and shells. They also carved glyphs into stucco, wood, and decorative stones such as jadeite. And they painted glyphs onto palace and temple wall murals considered so sacred that only

These glyphs represent a date: 9 *Ajaw*, 13 *Pop*.

the royals and priests were allowed to look at them. No matter where they left their mark, the scribes were after two things: preserving the history of their kings and making their kings look powerful.

Experts had been studying Maya hieroglyphs since Stephens and Catherwood published *Incidents of Travel in the Yucatán* in 1843. But it took more than 100 years for researchers to really understand the Mayan language. Scholars first discovered that some of the Maya symbols stood for periods of time. In 1958, a scholar by the name of Heinrich Berlin figured out that the glyphs identified specific places. Another scholar, Tatiana Proskouriakoff, was the first to prove that certain glyphs recorded the reigns of Maya kings. Until her discovery, experts assumed those glyphs were carvings of Maya gods. Finally, in 1973, experts succeeded in decoding the Mayan language. Today, experts know the meaning of 90 percent of Maya glyphs.

Glyphs representing the vowel "o."

Many of the hieroglyphs represent a single syllable. There are approximately 800 glyph symbols! Scribes strung words and sentences together by writing out combinations of these symbols. The scribes usually wrote sentences in this format: distance number-date-verb-object-subject. The distance number is a Calendar Round date and tells the reader the number of days, weeks, months, and years that occurred between an event described in the prior sentence and an event being described in a current sentence.

One reason it took experts so long to understand the Mayan language is because so many glyphs stood for the same syllable. For example, there are at least five different glyphs for the syllable *ba*! Also, many of the hieroglyphs are logograms. (A logogram is a written character that represents a word.) So, while some scribes used multiple glyphs to spell out a word phonetically, syllable by syllable, other scribes used a single glyph to represent a word.

Four of the glyphs that represent the syllable *ba*.

Top to bottom: glyphs for Pacal (or shield), bloodletter, and ball court.

Some scribes, for example, chose to write the name of Pacal the Great using the "shield" glyph because "Pacal" translates to "shield." Other scribes chose to spell his name out phonetically as "pa-cal-la." A good example of this difference, if applied to our society now, would be one person choosing to put six letters on a public restroom door to spell out "toilet" and another person deciding to put a simple stick figure of a man or woman on a restroom door.

Another thing that confused experts for a long time was that each scribe wrote the glyphs in his or her unique style. It took the experts a while to realize that glyphs that looked similar were, in fact, the same. It's like you and your brother or sister both drawing a cursive letter "B." Though they might look a little different, they are both the same letter of the alphabet.

All scribes used the same format to present their information, no matter what type of material they were writing on. They used a grid-style system of glyph blocks stacked together in pairs to make sentences. They wrote these sentences in vertical columns, from top to bottom and from left to right, completing each vertical column before moving to the top of the next column on the right. We follow the same format when we read our books and newspapers today.

When carving the glyphs into stelae, scribes first laid out their glyphs using ink. When they had the spacing right, they used wooden mallets and flint- or quartz-tipped tools to carve into the soft limestone.

The glyphs on the carved lintel to the right would be read left to right, two columns at a time.

Make Your Own

SOAP GLYPH CARVING

In this activity, you're going to carve the Maya glyph for *hu'un*, which means "book," making your own mini stela!

huun
book

1 Using the glyph symbol for "book" as your guide, use the ballpoint pen to lightly trace the design of the glyph onto your bar of soap. As the glyph is contained within a smooth-cornered square, the shape of your soap bar can represent the outside border of the glyph.

2 When you're happy with your design, use your pen to make the lines thick and deep.

3 Put a few drops of food coloring onto the top of a cotton swab. Use red or green, or mix them to make black. Run the swab through the grooved lines, making sure the color gets deep into the grooves.

4 Use a tissue to wipe any excess coloring off the surface of the soap, leaving the color only in your carved lines.

5 Display the glyph in your room—or use it during your next bath!

variation: Make several glyph carvings. Go to www.famsi.org/mayawriting/dictionary/mont-gomery/search.html and enter various words in the search engine—like the words for sun or day—to get the glyphs for those words. You can also download study guides with lots of hiero-glyphs on the same site at www.famsi.org/mayawriting/calvin/index.html.

SUPPLIES

rounded bar of bath soap
(can be full size or miniature)

ballpoint pen

food coloring

cotton swabs

tissue

pas
dawn

ak'ab
darkness

Make Your Own
PACAL THE GREAT BANNER

1 Cut the pillowcase into two equal rectangles, so you can make two banners. We're using white because surprise war raids often took place at night and we want Pacal's rivals to see the name of the king attacking them!

2 Slide the glyph stencils under the pillowcase, and position them where you want the glyphs to appear on the banner. You can use just one, or make border patterns by repeating the stencils. You should be able to clearly see the stencils through the pillowcase.

3 Trace the glyphs onto the pillowcase by copying the lines of the stencils. If you want the stencils bigger or smaller, you can enlarge or reduce them on a photocopy machine before you trace them onto the pillowcase.

4 Paint over your pencil lines with your paints. When the paints are dry, attach the sides of the banner to the wooden dowels with fabric glue or a hot glue gun.

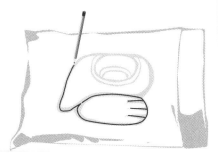

SUPPLIES

white pillow case

scissors

stencils of the Maya glyphs for "Pacal," "bloodletter," and "ball court" (see page 90)

pencil

craft paints—you choose the colors

paint brush for each color

2 wooden dowels (available in craft stores in 3-foot sections)

hot glue gun or fabric glue

CHAPTER 14

THE MAYA CODICES

Although scribes wrote in many different places, they spent most of their time writing in special books made of paper called **codices**. Within these books, scribes faithfully recorded centuries of Maya history, astronomical calculations, and religious practices. Some of the codices even recorded travel and hunting details. Others included tables for predicting when an eclipse of the sun would occur.

Of the thousands of codices created, only four remain today. That's because during the Spanish conquest of the Maya, Spanish soldiers burned the codices. Why? Because the Spanish thought the **pagan** codices were the work of the devil. Three of the codices eventually were found in European libraries. Experts believe

A Maya scribe working on a codex.

Pages from the Dresden Codex.

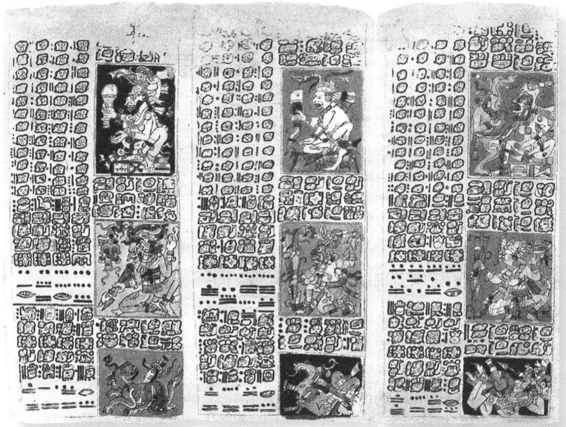

WORDS TO KNOW

codices: Handwritten books in which the Maya recorded their history. A single book is called a codex.

pagan: Work of someone who worships many gods.

horoscope: A prediction of a person's future based on the position of the planets and stars.

prophesies: Predictions for the future.

they ended up in Europe when Spanish explorers sent them home as souvenirs. Named after the cities where they are now located, these codices are known as the Dresden Codex, the Madrid Codex, and the Paris Codex.

The Dresden Codex, discovered in a private library in Vienna in 1739, discusses astronomy and includes tables for predicting solar eclipses. The Madrid Codex, found in Spain in the 1860s, includes **horoscopes** and **prophesies**. And the Paris Codex, discovered in 1859 at the Bibliothèque Nationale in Paris, highlights Maya rituals and ceremo-

WHY DID THE SPANISH BURN THE CODICES?

Diego de Landa (1524–1579), the Spanish priest in charge of converting the Maya to Christianity, ordered the burning of the Maya codices. As many of the writings were records of Maya religious ceremonies, de Landa considered them to be non-Christian and therefore evil. He burned thousands of the codices in huge bonfires. In his journal, de Landa wrote that the Maya were deeply upset that he had destroyed their written history. De Landa had his Catholic priests torture and kill any Maya who resisted conversion to Christianity. The priests whipped the Maya for worshipping their gods, scalded them with boiling water, and even stretched their joints with ropes and pulleys. More than 5,000 Maya were tortured and more than 150 died. De Landa also ordered the Maya temples torn down. Some Spanish priests were so upset at de Landa's treatment of the Maya that they turned against Spain.

nies. A fourth codex, called the Grolier Codex (because it was first displayed at the Grolier Club in New York City), may be a forgery. It talks about how the planet Venus affected Maya religion and astrology. Though no one knows where it was discovered, the Grolier Codex is now housed in Mexico City, Mexico.

Scribes couldn't buy paper from stores like we do today. They had to make their own from the bark of wild fig trees. It was a multistep process to turn the bark into paper. First, scribes stripped the inner bark from the wild fig trees and boiled it in lime water. The lime water softened the bark. After rinsing the bark in clean water, scribes pounded it with stone tools called *muinto* until it was very thin and wide.

They then layered sheets of this flattened bark on top of each other, alternately laying them horizontally and vertically, so the tree fibers crossed each other and made the paper strong and thick enough to be written on both sides. The paper was set to dry in the

DID YOU KNOW?

The ancient Maya made their codices in varying lengths. When folded, the Dresden Codex is only 3½ inches (9 cm) wide. But when its accordion-style pages are fully unfolded, it is nearly 12 feet long. This gave the scribes 74 folded pages to write on—or 2,268 inches. Folded, the Madrid Codex is only about 5 inches wide, but its 112 pages gave the scribes about 5,000 inches of writing space!

hot sun and then individual sheets were joined together, end to end, to make one long piece. The *muinto* would have made the beaten side of the paper rough, so scribes smoothed the paper with smooth, heated stones.

Scribes then used a wooden tool with a straight edge to crisply fold the paper back and forth on itself, like a fan or an accordion. The folded pages made it easy for scribes to open or close a book to the pages they wanted to see. But before they could write in the books, they needed to complete one more step: prepare the paper to absorb ink. To give the paper a smooth writing texture, scribes painted both sides of the pages with a layer of gesso, a thin plaster made from ground white limestone and water.

Mayan glyph for *write* or *paint*.

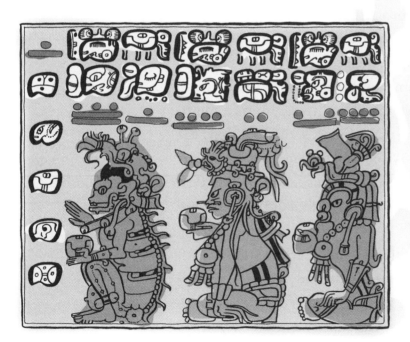

Page 13a of the Dresden Codex shows the gods of death, maize, and north (left to right), each holding the symbol for maize.

When the gesso was dry, the pages were refolded and the books covered in protective binders made from wood and jaguar pelts. Experts believe the protective covers were detachable. The covers were probably held in place with ties, not glue, and were placed on the codices when they were being read or written on, but removed when

Page 97b from the Madrid Codex illustrates the time of year for carving new masks.

the codices were stored. This belief is backed up by the fact that none of the four surviving codices have covers, and that archaeologists have uncovered many clay pots decorated with images of scribes writing in codices protected by covers made from jaguar pelts.

Just as the scribes used a grid when carving glyphs on other surfaces, they also used grid lines in their codices to plan the layout, as the books were too important (as well as time consuming to make) to mess up.

As they worked, scribes used brush pens (very thin brushes) and quills to apply ink to the book pages. Their brushes were made from different thicknesses of animal hair. Conch shells, cut lengthwise, served as ink pots! Black ink was made from soot and red ink from a mineral called hematite. Because Maya scribes used mostly black and red inks, the Aztec named the Maya lowlands the Land of Black and Red.

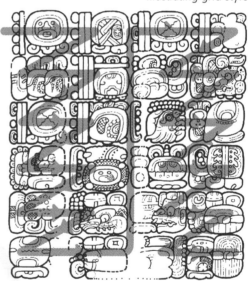

Mayan hieroglyphs in columns, illustrating grid-style system.

DID YOU KNOW?

Experts believe scribes made black ink for their codices by adding water to the soot scraped from the bottom of cooking pots. This soot is called carbon ink, and it is permanent, which is why epigraphers are still able to read the glyphs of the four Maya codices that survive today.

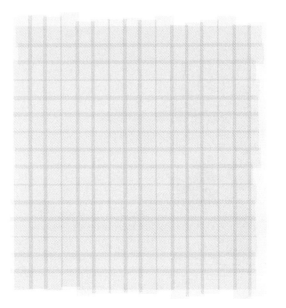

Make Your Own
PAPER

1 Mix the flour and the water in your pan. You can use the spoon, but your fingers will work just as well! Make sure you stir until there are no more clumps of flour. Set the pan aside.

2 Using the scissors, cut the paper into 1-inch-wide strips that are roughly the same length. (Don't worry if some of the pieces are longer than others; you can trim them off later.) Put the strips of paper in the flour and water mixture, and let them soak for several minutes. Make sure the pieces aren't sticking together. Move them around so each piece is covered in the mixture. While your paper soaks, spread out a piece of foil on a smooth, hard surface.

3 Next, carefully take the strips out, one at a time. Use your fingers to gently "squeegee" off the extra mixture. Lay half of the strips on the foil horizontally, making sure each piece slightly over-laps the one next to it. Lay the other half of the strips of paper vertically. When you are done, you should have two layers that are perpendicular to each other.

4 Lay a piece of foil on top of your paper strips. Roll the rolling pin over the foil. Push down firmly. (Some of the flour and water mixture may seep out at the sides.) After a few minutes of rolling, slowly pull back the top piece of foil. If some of the paper strips stick to it, gently pull them off and put them back down. (You don't need to roll them again.) Put your paper sheet, still on the bottom piece of foil, out in the sun to dry. Make sure it's on a flat surface. You can also leave it inside to dry, but it will just take a little longer.

5 When your paper is dry, carefully pull it away from the foil. Hold it up to the light. Notice the crisscross pattern? That's what the paper the Maya made looked like! Finally, trim the edges.

SUPPLIES

1 cup all-purpose flour

2 cups water

aluminum pan or any shallow dish

spoon

scissors

several sheets of unlined, white paper, any size

aluminum foil

rolling pin

Make Your Own
CODEX REPLICA

1 Lay one sheet of the paper on the table lengthwise in front of you. Use your ruler to measure in 9 inches from the left margin of the paper. Draw a vertical line for this measurement and cut along the line. Your paper now measures 8½ by 9 inches.

2 Use your ruler to measure 3 inches from the left edge, mark that spot with your pencil, then move your ruler 3 more inches to the right, and mark that spot. Your paper is now evenly divided into three 3-inch sections.

3 Lay your ruler vertically on the first 3-inch mark and carefully fold the paper over the left edge of the ruler. Move your ruler over to the 6-inch mark and fold the paper over again. You now have two hard creases. Refold the second crease in the opposite direction, under the sheet, so that the paper is folded like a fan.

4 Repeat these three steps for the second piece of paper. Connect the two pieces of paper using the Scotch tape. Make sure

the folds alternate in an accordion before you tape the two ends together.

5 You now have a single codex book. Your top sheet should open on the right, just like a printed book. You can flip through the codex page by page or you can fully lay it out so that all six pages are visible at once.

6 Now make the cover. Place the cardboard on the table lengthwise in front of you. Use your ruler to measure in 6¼ inches from the left edge. Draw a line for this measurement and cut along the line. You now have a piece of cardboard that is 8½ inches tall and 6¼ inches wide.

7 Fold the cardboard in half, so that you have a tall rectangle that is the same shape as your codex. Decorate the outside of the cover with your brown and black markers or paint it so that it looks like jaguar pelt or leather.

8 When the cover is finished (make sure the paint is dry), slip the codex pages into the cover. You can tie a ribbon around it to keep it closed.

SUPPLIES

2 pieces of 8½-by-11-inch white construction paper, or use the paper you made in the previous activity

ruler

pencil

scissors

clear Scotch tape

thin sheet of 8½-by-11-inch cardboard (the bottom of a writing pad works well)

black and brown markers or paint and paintbrush

ribbon

CHAPTER 15

ARTISTIC FLAIR

The art of the Maya flourished during the classic period because Maya kings liked to be surrounded by beautiful items that showed the wealth of their cities. Artists painted vibrant scenes of royal life on temple walls. Some of the items made by Maya artists were meant only for a king's tomb. One of the most beautiful tomb pieces found by archaeologists is a jadeite death mask. The artist who made it fitted many pieces of the hard, green stone together to represent the "ideal" Maya face. To the Maya, the most beautiful people had long oval heads, slightly slanting eyes, long curving noses, and fleshy lips.

Maya art focused primarily on the themes of blood sacrifices, war, and the deeds of great Maya rulers. The an-

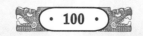

LOOKS THAT WERE IMPORTANT TO THE MAYA

The average height of an ancient Maya man was just over 5 feet; for women, it was 4 feet 8 inches. Typically, they had dark skin, dark eyes, and large noses that curved or hooked like an eagle's beak. The king and other nobles emphasized this feature by building the hook even higher with clay. The Maya worshipped *Yum-Kaax*, the god of corn, and they believed people were more attractive with elongated heads that resembled the shape of a corn stalk. To mold the heads of their babies into this long oval shape, they tied them to a board within several days of their birth. Another board was attached at an angle and the boards were brought together over the front of the head. The pressure of the boards was slowly increased over several days until the baby's skull was deformed. As the Maya nobles also valued crossed eyes, Maya mothers hung a piece of thread, weighted by a rubber ball or stone, between the infant's eyes, hoping they would permanently cross!

cient Maya did not think it was important to show happy families playing with their children, or laborers straining to build the great pyramids under the sweltering sun. Instead, art depicted special ceremonies, such as kings and queens cutting their bodies to offer their blood to the gods. Artists also liked to show war captives be-

Yum-Kaax, the god of corn.

Warriors with captives from a raiding party, from the murals at Bonampak, Chiapas, Mexico.

Stelae showing a king wearing a fancy outfit.

MANY ARTISTS WERE MEMBERS OF MAYA ROYAL FAMILIES, AND THEY OFTEN SIGNED THEIR NAMES ON THEIR WORK. IN FACT, THE MAYA REPRESENT THE ONLY MESOAMERICAN CULTURE IN WHICH ARTISTS TOOK CREDIT FOR THEIR INDIVIDUAL PIECES.

ing presented to victorious kings as they reclined on their thrones. They even painted the blood that dripped from prisoners as they were tortured by the king's warriors.

As the most important people in their cities, kings wanted to see their lives recorded. Stelae carvings were the primary way that kings displayed their power and accomplishments. Kings were always the central figures in the limestone and sandstone carvings, though they were often surrounded in the carvings by other people. Most artists carved figures in profile, facing left, and most ancient Maya carvings tend to look flat, rather than three-dimensional.

The often magnificent clothing of kings, priests, and other nobles is clearly visible in Maya carvings. The finely woven cloth used to make these clothes was produced by Maya weavers and embroiderers. For special ceremonies, weavers produced costumes for kings, priests, and nobles that were even more elaborate. Sometimes, the weavers even wove pearls and feathers right into material when it was intended for royal clothing.

A Maya ruler receiving a headdress.

THE POWERFUL JAGUAR

Jaguars look a lot like leopards, but their fur has bigger black-rimmed spots called rosettes. The Central American rainforests offer them plenty of cover as they stalk their prey. Jaguars have the strongest jaw of any cat found on the planet. They can easily bite through a turtle's shell or the skull of an animal. Because of their power, many Maya kings added "Jaguar" to their name, including Yaxchilán kings Shield Jaguar and Bird Jaguar.

Very few pieces of clothing made and worn by the ancient Maya survive today. Central America is so humid that fabrics deteriorate relatively quickly. Archaeologists have had to look at the clues left by Maya artists to discover how Maya royalty dressed. Wall frescos and pottery contain some of this information. Archaeologists know, for example, that during special ceremonies, kings wore headdresses decorated with jadeite, turquoise, and bird feathers and cloaks made from spotted jaguar pelts. The spotted pelts were prized by priests and kings because they believed the spots represented the stars and that jaguars helped them to communicate with the spirit world. Maya kings also believed that jaguars protected royal families.

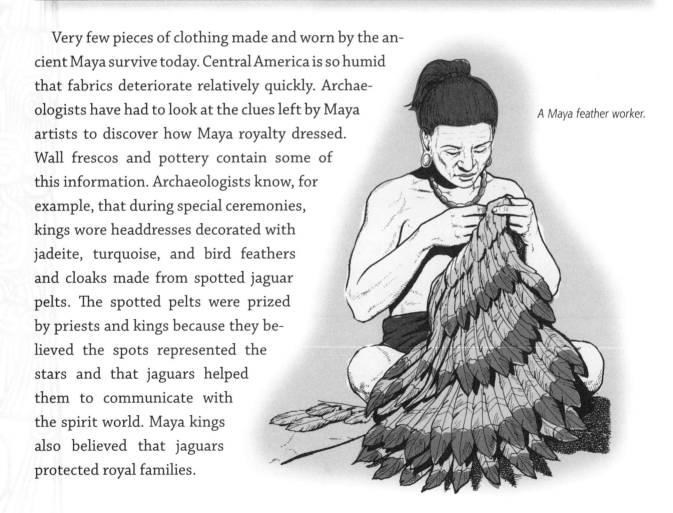

A Maya feather worker.

Make Your Own
ROYAL JAGUAR CAPE

1 Lay the square, light brown material on a table in front of you. Take the bottom edge and fold it up to the top edge so that you've made a rectangle. Take the left edge and fold it over to the right edge so that you once again have a square, only smaller.

fold

2 The bottom left corner is the center of your piece of material. This is where you'll cut your neck hole. Use your pencil to draw a rounded line about 2 inches out from the corner's point. Cut along this line.

fold

3 To make your cape's rounded shape, draw another rounded line, this time from the top left edge of your square down to the bottom right edge. Cut this rounded line. This line becomes the bottom edge of your cape.

cut along dotted lines

cut along dotted line

4 You've now got a poncho shape. But let's cut the cape so that it's open. Unfold the top fold of your cape once so that your cape has the shape of a full rainbow. Your neck hole is at the bottom and the rounded hem edge is at the top. Cut the fold that is to the left of the neck hole, along the bottom edge.

5 Now open the cape. Sew or staple the ties to the neck.

6 Study the photo of the jaguar, then cut similar shapes from your black felt and glue them to your cape. Use as few or as many spots as you like.

SUPPLIES

piece of light brown material approximately 1 yard by 1 yard—flannel works well because it doesn't need to be hemmed

ruler

pencil

scissors

two 6-inch lengths of brown ribbon

needle and thread OR stapler

black felt (enough to cover the cape with jaguar spots)

hot glue gun or fabric glue

CHAPTER 16

JEWELRY

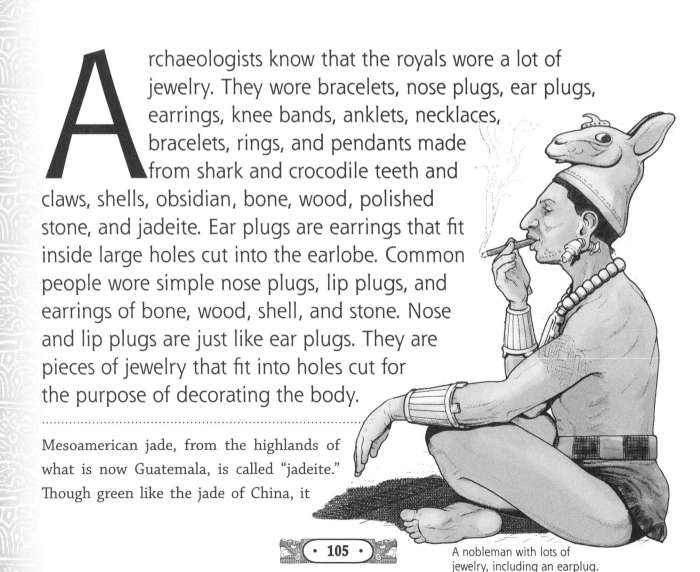

Archaeologists know that the royals wore a lot of jewelry. They wore bracelets, nose plugs, ear plugs, earrings, knee bands, anklets, necklaces, bracelets, rings, and pendants made from shark and crocodile teeth and claws, shells, obsidian, bone, wood, polished stone, and jadeite. Ear plugs are earrings that fit inside large holes cut into the earlobe. Common people wore simple nose plugs, lip plugs, and earrings of bone, wood, shell, and stone. Nose and lip plugs are just like ear plugs. They are pieces of jewelry that fit into holes cut for the purpose of decorating the body.

Mesoamerican jade, from the highlands of what is now Guatemala, is called "jadeite." Though green like the jade of China, it

A nobleman with lots of jewelry, including an earplug.

THE MAYA DID NOT USE GOLD OR COPPER IN THEIR DECORATIVE ITEMS UNTIL THEIR POST-CLASSIC PERIOD (900–1524 CE), WHEN THEY BEGAN ACCEPTING IT IN TRADE WITH THE AZTEC. THE AZTEC VALUED GOLD JEWELRY AS MUCH AS THE MAYA VALUED JEWELRY MADE FROM JADEITE.

Jadeite earplugs.

can also be black. Maya royalty prized jadeite because its green color reminded them of fields of green corn stalks. Jadeite is a very hard stone that ranges in color from blue-green to nearly black. The Maya collected it from the riverbeds of what is now Guatemala. Because they prized it so much, Maya nobles even drilled holes in their teeth and filled them with jadeite! The Maya learned how to drill, grind, and cut jadeite from the Olmec people. Because jadeite is so hard, it takes great skill to carve—especially without metal tools. Flint, which the Maya used for cutting and carving limestone, was useless against jadeite. But the ancient Maya were able to saw jadeite into flat slabs by drawing a cord embedded with quartz pieces back and forth over its surface with the help of water and sand. They used bone drills to make decorative cuts and plant fibers to polish the surface of the stone. Jewelry and other items made out of jadeite have been found in Maya tombs.

Jadeite necklace with pendant.

Make Your Own
REPLICA OF A ROYAL MAYA JADEITE NECKLACE

In this activity, you'll make a replica of a jadeite burial necklace found in a royal tomb at Calakmul, a Maya city in the lowland rainforest. You'll make your "jadeite" out of green Sculpey clay.

Note: Sculpey clay is safe to handle, but you should not use your cooking or eating utensils for making and baking the clay.

1 Notice that the Maya necklace pictured on the next page is made of a mixture of round and elongated beads. It also contains a large rectangular-shaped decorative centerpiece. You will make all these pieces from clay before you assemble your necklace.

2 Prepare your work space by covering a table in newspaper. Cover this with enough wax paper to give you room to roll out your beads. Or roll out your clay on an 8-by-10-inch glazed tile. The tile works well because the clay doesn't stick to it.

SUPPLIES

newspaper

wax paper OR 8-by-10-inch glazed ceramic tile

elastic thread (green or white)

ruler

scissors

masking tape

plastic knife or clay modeling tool

Sculpey clay (green, black, white)

rolling pin

toothpicks (the heavy round kind)

index cards

wooden skewers

disposable foil trays

3 Measure out a piece of elastic thread that is long enough for the centerpiece to sit below your collar bone. Use the masking tape to tape both ends of this piece to your workspace. It will show you how many beads to make. Remember to leave a couple of inches of extra elastic thread on each end to tie the knot.

4 Decide which color of clay you want to use. Mix them, if you like. Green with half as much black makes dark green. Equal amounts of green and white makes light green. Or you can use pearl white to make pearl green. After choos-

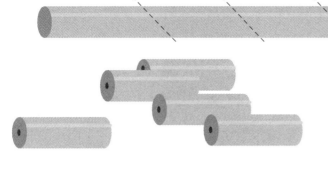

ing your colors, make your beads. Make round beads by rolling a small piece of clay in the palms of your hands. To make your rectangle beads, roll a piece of clay into a smooth ball. Shape the ball into a long log. Roll this log on your wax paper or ceramic tile to make a long coil. Press gently so it remains even. Cut the beads into the desired lengths.

5 Carefully poke holes through the beads with a toothpick. So that you don't squash the bead, poke the toothpick halfway through from one side, then halfway through from the other side, then all the way through. Make sure the hole is large enough for your elastic thread to easily fit through.

6 To make the rectangular centerpiece, draw a pattern on an index card and cut it out. Roll out a ¼-inch-thick piece of clay big enough for this piece. Cut away any extra clay. Cut the "T" shape into the center of the piece, making it as large as you like. Use a toothpick to make a hole through this bead at the top

and bottom just like you did for the smaller beads.

7 To bake your beads, thread them on the wooden skewers. Don't allow them to touch. Cut slots on both sides of the long sides of the foil pan and lay the skewers in the slots. Put your bead centerpiece on an index card and place it in the foil pan. The card keeps it from sticking. Bake per the directions on the clay's packaging. Most polymer clays are baked at 275 degrees Fahrenheit (130 degrees Celsius). Remember that Sculpey clay does NOT harden until it is completely cool.

8 When your pieces are cool, thread the elastic through the top holes in your centerpiece so the elastic runs across the back. With the thread even on both sides, add an equal number of beads to each side. When you get to the end of the thread, tie the ends together.

9 Cut another piece of elastic thread for the bottom of the necklace. Thread it through the bottom holes. When it is even on both sides, add more beads. Tie knots at each end to secure the beads.

CHAPTER 17

POTTERY

Maya artists produced world-class pottery. To make their pottery, the ancient Maya used clay from the riverbeds. They strengthened it by adding calcite, quartz, or volcanic ash. The artists made clay pots for cooking, storing food, and for religious and medical purposes. Some of their pots were 5 feet high! Experts believe that the better quality pieces were made in the palace courts.

Maya potters used clay coils to build their pots, which was a slow process. After building the coils up as high as they wanted, they smoothed the coils together with their fingers. They also used clay slabs to make ceramic boxes. Potters may have used a device called

The steps for making a coil pot.

A Maya artist painting pottery.

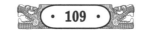

a *k'abal*, which is a wooden platform that is rotated with the feet. Much like a potter's wheel is today, the *k'abal* would have been a big help to potters, allowing them to work on all sides of their piece without having to lift up the pot or change their sitting position.

To bake their unglazed pieces, Maya potters used low-temperature ovens heated by wood fires. These were often pits in the ground. To decorate the pottery with scenes of court life, ceramists used slip paint, which is a mixture of finely ground pigment, clay, and water. The heat of the ovens would have destroyed many of the dyes the potters could have used to decorate their pottery. So they used just a few colors that could stand up to the heat. These included black made from manganese, yellows and browns made from limonite, and oranges and reds made from hematite. These minerals are common throughout the Mesoamerican rainforest today.

Examples of Maya vases.

Potters usually outlined figures of animals and people in black, and used the yellows, browns, reds, and oranges to fill the figures in. The artists who painted the pottery made their paint brushes by attaching animal hair bristles to a hollow tube. They also used yucca fibers, which were easily pulled out of the yucca leaves like strands of thread. To give their pieces a high gloss finish, experts believe Maya artists rubbed the pieces with a resin.

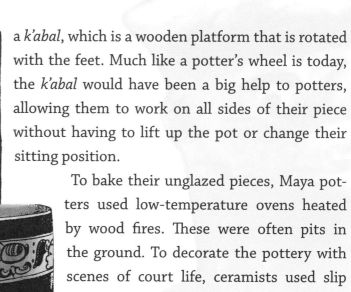

A Maya urn.

Make Your Own
CLAY DRINKING CUP

1 Create an easy-to-clean work surface by taping a piece of wax paper to a table or countertop.

2 Make the cup's base by rolling a chunk of clay out flat with a rolling pin. Cut out a round circle using your cookie cutter.

3 Form a long coil by rolling a piece of clay between your palms. Keep the coil the same thickness along its length, so that your finished cup is even.

4 Place the coil along the outer edge of the round base. Use additional coils to build up the sides of the cup until it is 3 or 4 inches high.

5 To make the sides of the cup smooth, dip your fingers into your bowl of water and use

the liquid to smooth the coils together. Or you can keep the coil look if you like its texture.

6 Use the toothpick to draw diamond patterns into the surface of the cup. Let your cup air dry.

SUPPLIES

wax paper

masking tape

air-hardening clay **OR** paper-clay (available in craft stores)

plastic knife or art tool

rolling pin

round cookie cutter

small bowl of water

toothpick (optional)

acrylic paints

7 If you want, you can use acrylic paints to decorate the OUTSIDE of the cup with glyphs or color in the pattern.

GLOSSARY

A

agave: A type of cactus plant that grows in Central America. The Maya used it for its sisal fibers.

ah kin: A Maya high priest.

Ah Mun: The Maya god of maize (corn).

ahaw: The Maya word for "lord," "ruler," or "high king."

aqueduct: A pipe or channel designed to transport water from a one place to another—water flows through the aqueduct by force of gravity.

archaeologist: Someone who studies ancient people and their cultures.

astronomy: The study of the stars and planets. The Maya were expert astronomers.

atanzahob: A Maya matchmaker or marriage broker.

B

bedrock: The solid rock earth, well beneath the softer surface of soil, sand, clay, gravel, or water.

C

cacao: A rainforest tree that produces a cacao bean. Maya kings loved the bitter chocolate drink from these beans.

Calendar Round: A calendar of 52 years that is the made up of the Sacred Round and the Vague Year.

cau-uchu: The Maya term for the rubber trees they used to make Pok-A-Tok balls and other items. The translation is "weeping wood."

chicle: The sap of a sapodilla tree, which the Maya chewed after it hardened. It is still used to make chewing gum.

codices: Handwritten books in which the Maya recorded their history. A single book is called a codex. Only three originals remain.

colonist: A new settler or founder of a colony who is originally from somewhere else.

commoners: Most of the people in Maya society. Commoners were those who were not kings, other royalty, priests, merchants, government officials, or the wealthy.

conch shells: Large spiral shells that can be used as horns.

conquistador: Sixteenth-century Spanish soldiers who conquered and enslaved the Maya.

copal: A kind of sap that comes from tropical trees and is used in candles.

corbel arches: An arch-like structure in which the sides are formed by an overlapping arrangement of bricks or stones where each tier extends farther out from the wall than the tier below.

crop rotation: Growing a different crop each year on the same piece of land, and letting a piece of land rest every few years.

D

drought: A period of little or no rain that causes extensive damage to crops or prevents them from growing at all.

E

epigraphers: Experts who study ancient writings.

F

fasting: To eat very little or nothing at all for a period of time. The Maya usually did this for religious purposes.

fetishes: Small figurines that are believed to have magical or spiritual powers.

frescoes: Works of art painted with pigments onto plaster before it dries.

G

glyph: A symbolic figure or a character usually carved in stone. Also the basic unit in the Maya system of writing.

gnarled: Twisted and deformed.

god: A superhuman being that is worshipped.

gourds: The dried and hollowed-out shell of plants related to the pumpkin, squash, and cucumber.

H

haab or Vague Year: The 365-day year of the Maya calendar.

hand loom: A loom on which the yarn is stretched between two horizontal sticks attached to an "A"-shaped frame, similar in construction to an easel.

headdress: An elaborate covering for the head worn during ceremonial occasions.

hearth: The floor of a fire or oven.

hieroglyphs: A writing system in which pictures and symbols represent meaning or sounds or a combination of the two. One symbol is called a glyph.

horoscope: A prediction of a person's future based on the position of the planets and stars.

huipil: A loose cotton dress worn by Maya women from the beginnings of Maya civilization to the present.

I

indigo: An intense blue dye obtained from a particular type of shrub or herb, or produced synthetically.

J

jadeite: A rare and prized mineral, usually emerald to light green, used by the Maya to make jewelry.

K

k'in: A day in the Maya calendar.

L

limestone: A rock that the Maya used to build roads, temples, and other important buildings. Underground it is soft, but it hardens with exposure to air.

loincloth: A strip of cloth worn around the mid-section of the body.

Long Count: A complex calendar only used by Maya priests and scribes (because it was so challenging to understand) to record very long periods of time—even from the start of creation.

M

maize: Corn.

memba unicoob: The Maya word for common worker.

merchant: A buyer and seller of different items for profit.

Mesoamerica: The area in Central America that made up the Maya homeland. Today this land is divided up into the countries of Mexico, Guatemala, Belize, and Honduras.

millennium: A period of 1,000 years.

N

nomads: A group of people who move from location to location according to the seasons in search of food, water, hunting land, etc.

P

pagan: Work of someone who worships many gods.

pati: A shawl worn by the Maya women over their shoulders.

pelt: An animal skin.

pentacoob: The Mayan word for "slaves."

plumb bob: A weight on the end of a line, used especially by masons and carpenters to establish exact vertical and horizontal lines.

Pok-A-Tok: A Maya ball game played for fun and during special religious ceremonies. Losing team members sometimes lost their heads or were sacrificed during blood offerings to the gods.

polytheism: The worship of multiple gods. The Maya had to appease many gods.

pom: The resin of the copal tree. The Maya harvested it for rubber and incense.

Popul Vuh: The "Maya Bible" that tells the story of how the Maya were fashioned by the gods from corn.

pre-Columbian: A term that refers to the time period before the Indian civilizations living in Mesoamerica encountered Europeans.

priest: A person with special religious status who performed sacrifices and rituals, and took care of the spiritual needs of society.

procession: A group of people moving along in the same direction, to the same place, or for the same reason.

prophesies: Predictions for the future.

pyramid: Specific to Mesoamerican cultures like the Maya, these were four-sided structures, typically used as temples, with steep, stepped sides and a flat top. Blood sacrifices were often conducted on the flat tops and the bodies then thrown down the steps.

quarry: To dig or cut rock from the earth.

quetzal: A bird prized by Maya kings for its brilliant blue-green feathers. Today this bird faces extinction.

quills: Pens made of feathers.

rainforest: Any dense, tropical forest with a yearly rainfall of at least 100 inches (2.5 meters).

reservoir: A natural or artificial pond or lake used to store and regulate the supply of water.

Sacred Round: The Maya count-of-days calendar; based on 20-day months.

sacrifice: An offering to a god.

scribe: A member of Maya society who wrote with hieroglyphs on many types of surfaces, as well as in codices, to keep records of all kinds.

self-mutilation: Injury or disfigurement to oneself.

shaman-priest: A priest-doctor in Maya society who tended to the physical needs of the people. The shaman-priest used magic, sorcery, and medicines made from plants and the natural world, for healing, divination, and control over natural events.

sisal: Stiff fibers from the agave leaves used by the Maya to make rope and many other things.

slip paint: A mixture of finely ground pigment, clay, and water painted onto pottery.

spindle whorl: A rod or pin, tapered at one end and usually weighted at the other, on which fibers are spun into thread and then wound.

stelae: Vertical slabs of stone that the Maya used to record dates and important information about their rulers. Most are between 3 and 23 feet tall. Maya artists used stone chisels and wooden hammers to carve symbols into the stone.

stucco: A durable finish for exterior walls, usually composed of cement, sand, limestone, and water, that is applied while wet.

terraces: Level areas cut into a steep slope to provide a flat section for crops.

thatch: Durable plant stalks, such as reeds or palm strips, used for roofing.

tumpline: A strap slung over the forehead or chest and used for carrying or helping to support a load being hauled on a one's back.

tun: A year in the Maya solar calendar.

***tzolk'in* or Sacred Round**: A period of 260 days constituting a complete cycle of all the permutations of 20 day names with the numbers 1 to 13 that constitutes the Maya sacred year.

uayeb: The five unlucky days in the Maya's 365-day *haab* calendar.

underworld (*Xibalbá*): The home of the dead, as well as some of the evil gods.

Vague Year: The Maya calendar based on 20-day months; combines with the Sacred Round to create the Calendar Round.

witz: The Maya word for "mountain." Maya temples were built to represent witz.

Yucatán: The home of the early Maya, before they spread to other areas of Mesoamerica (to Guatemala, Belize, Honduras, and other provinces of Mexico).

RESOURCES

Books

Ancona, George. *Mayeros: A Yucatec Maya Family*. New York: Lothrop, Lee & Shepard Books, 1997.

Coulter, Laurie. *Secrets in Stone: All About Maya Hieroglyphs*. Ontario: Little, Brown and Company, 2001.

Day, Nancy. *Your Travel Guide to Ancient Mayan Civilization*. Minneapolis, MN: Runestone Press, 2001.

Gerson, Mary-Joan. *People of Corn: A Mayan Story*. Ontario: Little, Brown and Company, 1995.

Kallen, Stuart. *The Mayans*. San Diego: Lucent Books, Inc., 2001.

Laughton, Timothy. *The Maya: Life, Myth and Art*. London: Duncan Baird Publishers, 1998.

Lourie, Peter. *The Mystery of the Maya: Uncovering the Lost City of Palenque*. Honesdale, PA: Boyds Mill Press, Inc., 2001.

Macdonald, Fiona. *Step into the Aztec and Mayan Worlds*. London: Lorenze Books, 1998.

Morton, Lyman. *Yucatán Cook Book: Recipes and Tales*. Santa Fe, NM: Red Crane Books, Inc., 1996.

Netzley, Patricia. *Maya Civilization*. San Diego: Lucent Books, Inc., 2002.

Orr, Tamra. *The Maya*. Danbury, CT: Watts Library, 2005.

Polin, C. J. *The Story of Chocolate*. New York: DK Publishing, Inc., 2005.

Sharer, Robert J. *Daily Life in Maya Civilization*. Westport, CT: Greenwood Press, 1996.

Schuman, Michael A. *Mayan and Aztec Mythology*. Berkeley Heights, New Jersey: Enslow Publishers, Inc., 2001.

Whitlock, Ralph. *Everyday Life of the Maya*. New York: Dorsett Press, 1976.

Web Sites

CultureFocus.Com: www.culturefocus.com/guatemala.htm. Beautiful photos of Maya ruins.

Florida International University Libraries: www.fiu.edu/~library/internet/subjects/maya.html. Tons of information on Maya history, culture, and inventions.

Jaguar Sun: www.jaguar-sun.com. This is a great web site by Jeeni Criscenzo, author of a novel about the Maya called *Place of Mirrors*.

Mayan Kids: http://mayankids.com/mmkglossary/!glossary_a.htm. Lots of information, including an extensive glossary of Maya words.

Native American Indian Resources: www.kstrom.net/isk/maya/mayastor.html. Visit here to read traditional Maya tales.

PBS: www.pbs.org/wgbh/nova/maya/world.html.

Science Museum of Minnesota's Maya Adventure: www.smm.org/sln/ma/chiapas.html. Information and drawings of clothing worn by the Chiapas Maya currently living in Mexico. Many links to other Maya information.

INDEX